DENNIS O'DRISCOLL

New and Selected
Poems

ANVIL PRESS POETRY

Published in 2004
by Anvil Press Poetry Ltd
Neptune House 70 Royal Hill London SE10 8RF
www.anvilpresspoetry.com
Reprinted in 2005, 2006

This book is published with financial assistance
from Arts Council England

Designed and set in Monotype Ehrhardt by Anvil
Printed and bound in England
by Cromwell Press, Trowbridge, Wiltshire

ISBN 0 85646 373 6

A catalogue record for this book
is available from the British Library

Online Services
www.kingston.gov.uk

THE ROYAL BOROUGH OF
KINGSTON
UPON THAMES

Renew a book (5 times)	Request a book
Change of address	Email a branch
Library news and updates	Get your PIN
Search the catalogue	Access reference sites

New Malden Library
48 Kingston Road
New Malden
KT3 3LY

020 8547 5006
newmalden.library@kingston.gov.uk

By Dennis O'Driscoll

For Patrick Lannan and Thomas Lynch

– who raise spirits –

ACKNOWLEDGEMENTS

As well as previously uncollected poems, *New and Selected Poems* includes work from the following collections: *Kist* (Dolmen Press, 1982), *Hidden Extras* (Anvil Press/Dedalus Press, 1987), *Long Story Short* (Anvil Press/Dedalus Press, 1993), *Quality Time* (Anvil Press, 1997), *Weather Permitting* (Anvil Press, 1999) and *Exemplary Damages* (Anvil Press, 2002). 'The Bottom Line' was originally published in a limited-edition booklet (Dedalus Editions No. 5, 1994).

For first publication of poems in this book, grateful acknowledgement is made to the following: *Agenda, Atlanta Review, Columbia, The Echo-Room, Harvard Review, The Irish Times, Irish University Review, James Joyce Bloomsday Magazine, London Magazine, London Review of Books, Metre, New England Review, New Hibernia Review, New Statesman, The North, Oxford Poetry, The Paris Review, PN Review, Poetry* (Chicago), *Poetry International, Poetry Ireland Review, Poetry London, Poetry Review, Princeton University Library Chronicle, Quadrant, The Recorder, Sibila, The Southern Review, The Sunday Independent, The Sunday Times, The Sunday Tribune, Thumbscrew, Times Literary Supplement, TriQuarterly* and *The Yale Review*. Many of the poems were broadcast on RTE Radio and Television. A Lannan Literary Award (1999) and an Arts Council/An Chomhairle Ealaíon bursary (2004) were vital supports.

Warm thanks to Peter Jay for keeping the flame in the forge; also to Kit Yee Wong, Hamish Ironside and Robert Towers, friends around the Anvil.

Contents

from Kist (1982)

from Hidden Extras (1987)

from Long Story Short (1993)

The Bottom Line (1994)   89

from Quality Time (1997)

Foreseeable Futures (2004)

FROM

Kist

(1982)

Someone

someone is dressing up for death today, a change of skirt or tie
eating a final feast of buttered sliced pan, tea
scarcely having noticed the erection that was his last
shaving his face to marble for the icy laying out
spraying with deodorant her coarse armpit grass
someone today is leaving home on business
saluting, terminally, the neighbours who will join in the cortege
someone is paring his nails for the last time, a precious moment
someone's waist will not be marked with elastic in the future
someone is putting out milkbottles for a day that will not come
someone's fresh breath is about to be taken clean away
someone is writing a cheque that will be rejected as 'drawer deceased'
someone is circling posthumous dates on a calendar
someone is listening to an irrelevant weather forecast
someone is making rash promises to friends
someone's coffin is being sanded, laminated, shined
who feels this morning quite as well as ever
someone if asked would find nothing remarkable in today's date
perfume and goodbyes her final will and testament
someone today is seeing the world for the last time
as innocently as he had seen it first

Kist

On this lovers' morning, our hearts chime.
Later, the slow death knell of hers
and a coffin door slamming
in her last chill breath.

Preparing me for your
death, strands of silver,
coffin-handle bright,
thread your oak-brown hair.

And, as I pace behind the hearse,
my own face in its glass
takes on the wrinkled grain
of coffin wood.

(14 February 1975)

Siblings

I am writing at exactly the moment
you sent me the message of his death
precisely this time last year.

Returning home from school to an empty house,
you learn the vulnerability of those
who know how thin the barrier of flesh is,

that looking forward becomes looking back
until there is nothing either way but death.
It is quiet in the office as I write,

hiding this paper under a file,
heat rising from radiators, someone whistling,
someone listing soccer scores.

We have spent a year without him – his thoughts
scattered, his burden of organs eased.
This is just another working day here

of queries, letters, tea-breaks, forms.
Any minute now some telephone will ring
but I do not dread its news, as then.

I concentrate upon this moment, cup it in my hands,
to understand what you have lost in these
past years as home became an orphanage

and you soiled the carpet in the hall
with the clay of their two burials,
your world refracted by a lens of tears.

Traces

I

time sieves us into dust
our residue is gall–stone, bone
flesh offers no protection
elbow and back wear through its fabric

II

beneath the surface of our lives
skin deep is buried death
(like underwear we carry skeletons
folded neatly in our trunks)

III

its name is signed
between lines of forehead
in calligraphy of ribs
shakily on wet cardiogram, last will

IV

even from padded cells of brain
life eventually escapes
bones like scaffolding mark sites
where flesh walls stood

Porlock

this is the best poem I have never written
it is composed of all the stunning lines I thought up
but lacked the time or place or paper to jot down

this is a poem of distractions, interruptions, clamouring telephones
this is a poem that reveals how incompatible with verse my life is
this is a home for mentally lapsed poems

this is the lost property office of poetry
this is my poem without a hero, conceived but never born
this is a prisoner of consciousness, a victim of intelligence leaks

this is the poem that cannot learn itself by heart
this is the poem that has not found its individual voice
this is the poem that has forgotten its own name

this is my most unmemorable creation
these are my most disposable lines
this is the poem that dispenses with words

Wings

like tumbling masonry pigeons topple from a building
magpies flock for gold to where sun gilds a tree

the heron paddles with its skirts rolled up
lapwings at their air base wear a crew cut

thrushes pluck a field's loose threads
kettle swans simmer on electric rings

a team of wild geese rows across the evening cheering
and an exhibitionist bat opens a mackintosh

the hawk plays darts, the swallows skate
the drunken cuckoo hiccups one last time

then night's television screen of stars is switched on
a murder story with the owl's loud screams

Miracles

I *Cana*

Making a chalice
of the glass
he wounded water,

keeping his blood,
his good wine,
until last.

II *Desert*

Loaves were multiplied
so that the poor
would eat their fill.

Beneath bread's crusted dome,
freshly each day,
he chose to come.

III *Calvary*

An icicle,
his frozen body drips.

Our wrongs rust
his forgiving palms.

His death, a red sunset,
brings the next day fair.

Flatland

Take-away foods, small late-night stores,
record dealers, posters for Folk Mass.
Coke and fried chicken make an ideal meal here,
unpacked in a bedsitter and swallowed near a one-bar fire.

Down bicycle-cluttered corridor, by coinbox telephone,
special-offer leaflets, buff uncollected post,
weekends open optimistically beforehand
like sands of package holiday brochures.

Falling plaster bares ceiling laths, like piano keys
stripped of their ivory; fireplaces are blocked.
Revolving record wheels, slow music after pubs,
will transport lovers into a seagull-velvet dawn,

into stale cigarette smoke, lingering tastes of beer;
outside, ivy-bearded trees conceal the rubbish bins;
milk cartons roll through long-haired lawns;
the hall door buttoned with bells.

In neat gardens on the next street, wickerwork branches
will be baskets plump with fruit yet.
Couples yawn and part. Sunday now,
the heavy hours weigh down the watch's scales

to 4 o'clock, sports programmes on the radio,
as evening's cigarette-butt is stubbed out,
leaving an ash-grey sky
which only a working Monday will illuminate.

FROM

Hidden Extras

(1987)

Middle-Class Blues

He has everything.
A beautiful young wife.
A comfortable home.
A secure job.
A velvet three-piece suite.
A metallic-silver car.
A mahogany cocktail cabinet.
A rugby trophy.
A remote-controlled music centre.
A set of golf clubs under the hallstand.
A fair-haired daughter learning to walk.

What he is afraid of most
and what keeps him tossing some nights
on the electric underblanket,
listening to the antique clock
clicking with disapproval from the landing,
are the stories that begin:
He had everything.
A beautiful young wife.
A comfortable home.
A secure job.
Then one day.

Here and Now

There's a mirror that has seen me for the last time
           – BORGES

There are poems I could write only in present tense
that I will never be in a position to again:
about looking into a mirror and seeing not one grey hair
or sitting with you in an unburgled living room,
the terminal diseases still dormant in our cells.

There is the poem of this very moment,
sunset streaking the horizon like a circus poster,
a v-neck of geese homing from stubble,
thistle fleece rising like soap bubbles,
a wasp in jockey colours racing the dark.

There is the poem of this unrecorded second,
so nondescript, so tame, so plain:
the smack of a gardener's spade, a distracting hum,
radio jingles leaching through a parked car;
and now a milkman's helper is distributing bills.

Somewhere else, locked in our past tense, beyond grasp,
first lovers thrill to mutual discoveries:
beginnings we too recall, pristine invigorating dawns
fresh as if earth's architect just left,
cloud's mortar setting above building-rubble hills.

And elsewhere, too, a world of frenzy: commodity markets,
blackberry riot police, crises of age and youth.
The unwrinkled glass that holds me in the balance
between past and future is a river I must cross,
floating out of depth towards its unreflective side.

Reader's Digest *Family Medical Adviser*

'An A–Z Guide to Everyday Ailments'

Everyday asthma and brain tumour.
Everyday chilblains, cancers, coronaries.
Everyday depression and epilepsy.
Everyday falls and gallstones.
Everyday Hodgkin's disease and insomnia.
Everyday jaundice, keratosis, leukaemia.
Everyday multiple sclerosis, nephritis, ovarian cyst.
Everyday polio, pneumonia, quinsy, rheumatic pain.
Everyday syphilis, threadworm, ulcer, varicose vein.

Six hundred and twenty-four pages long.
Three columns wide.
One size fits all.

Two Silences

I

his morning calls over, my father drives outside the town
he parks beside a rusty gate tied with baling twine
shy daisies eye me from a lush coat of green
we unpack lunch with the windows down
the sandwiches my mother made taste creamy and fresh
we dine in perfect silence
I smell the dark vapour from his coffee flask
and drink tickling lemonade from a chipped cup
there are slices of chocolate swiss-roll for dessert
and a banana ripening into cheetah spots
a breeze brings goosebumps to the barks
of trees that toss their heads of leaves back
to form chintzy lampshades for the sun
we take our ease, breadcrumbs hardening in our laps

II

my father was turning away from life exiled in pain
harder to locate with each hospital visit
drumming sonatas of impatience on a bedside locker
shuffling among dressing-gowned wraiths
whose slippers had worn the corridor linoleum to a blur:
after he was granted access to his day-clothes
I searched the gloomy wood-panelled billiard-room
and the tacky shop of evening papers, Get Well cards
a summer shower was drooping at the time I found him
on a remote bench beneath a protrusive tree
ground staff clattered past with rake and barrow
in the recreation hall the chaplain would be tuning the TV
out at sea the mail boat was dissolving into mist
as I came near he turned the other way

Siblings Revisited

1 *Declan at Twenty*

Only a few years ago, it was Jennings schoolboy stories
that I brought you. Now, I pack avant-garde books:
Tom Mallin, Alan Burns, a B.S. Johnson play.

'There isn't enough enthusiasm in the world', you tell me.
And yours is revealed, petitioning for the release of prisoners,
contributing a series entitled 'Freedom' to *The Tipperary Star*,
reading African novelists, surveying a heron's nest,
displaying your unframed paintings along the bedroom wall.
In one corner, where a cliff of rock magazines used rise,
back issues of *New Statesman* pile – the town's sole subscriber.
Of late, you have taken to playing the trumpet,
scorning sheet music in favour of the improvised tune.

You were maturing, swelling with cells, as parental death loomed,
called twice from the classroom for grim news.
I hint at the advantages of further studies sometimes.
Without success. And out of your seasonal job, of bog work,
you pay for essentials: subscriptions, membership fees, jazz LPs.
On blustery days, I wonder if the wind is with or against you
as you cycle there, along unsheltered miles . . .

Play me, improvise on the trumpet, the rhythm of your new life.
Blast me the notes of your freedom.
Show me how to extend past experience to joy.

II *Eithne at Eighteen*

The local paper carries your photograph this week,
at work collating parish registers of baptisms and marriages.
But death is the category you first kept records of.

I remember you waiting in the spacious hospital lobby,
too young to visit our mother's cancer ward
though old enough to know the worst.
Then growing up to watch our father's graph
decline so rapidly towards the grave;
to buy school clothes with an executor's cheque.

Flush with saved earnings from your temporary job now,
you can afford to join me in the city for a day trip,
greeting me with the smile of the unvanquished,
trying on endless styles in department store cubicles.

You edge your way into the world with relish,
needing only a little support at this stage,
wanting only to channel your ardency
into one of the scores of jobs you patiently apply for
while vast untapped talent drains down the dole queues.

Enjoy the long evenings of these first post-school days.
Sleep well in our parents' ample bed.
That smile you surrender generously
has been achieved against the greatest odds.

Disarmament

your first grey hairs
are picked off readily enough
and harmony restored

that metal sheen proliferates
and you risk baldness
as you eliminate invaders

Stillborn

What we are lamenting
Is what has not been
And what will not have seen
This mild May morning.

What we are lamenting
Is unsuckled air
And what was brought to bear
This mild May morning.

What we are lamenting
Is our flesh and blood, this child
That has not laughed or cried
This mild May morning.

What we are lamenting
Is the life we crave
Snatched from the cradle to the grave
This mild May morning.

Normally Speaking

To assume everything has meaning.
To return at evening
feeling you have earned a rest
and put your feet up
before a glowing TV set and fire.
To have your favourite shows.
To be married to a local
whom your parents absolutely adore.
To be satisfied with what you have,
the neighbours, the current hemline,
the dual immersion, the government doing its best.
To keep to an average size
and buy clothes off the rack.
To bear the kind of face
that can be made-up to prettiness.
To head contentedly for work
knowing how bored you'd be at home.
To book holidays to where bodies blend,
tanned like sandgrains.
To be given to little excesses:
Christmas hangovers, spike high heels,
chocolate eclair binges, lightened hair.
To postpone children until the house extension
can be afforded and the car paid off.
To see the world through double glazing
and find nothing wrong.
To expect to go on living like this
and to look straight forward. No regrets.
To get up each day neither in wonder nor in fear,
meeting people on the bus you recognise
and who accept you, without question, for what you are.

What She Does Not Know Is

That she is a widow.
That these are the last untinged memories of her life.
That he is slumped in his seat at a lay-by.
That a policeman is trying to revive him.
That the knife and fork she has set are merely decorative.
That the steak beside the pan will go to waste.
That he has lost his appetite.
That the house she is tidying is for sale.
That the holiday snap will be used for his memorial card.
That he will not be subjected to direct light again.
That she will spend all night brewing tears.
That it is not his car she will soon hear slowing down outside.

Serving Time

Fulfilling the forecast on the breakfast radio,
pods of hail were shelled on window ledges.
A wind that would whittle headstones
down to bones still rages as this poem
comes to you live from the second floor.
I take my place in the commentary box.

Here we all congregate at public hatch and desk:
the skinny spectacled clerk
with the Tupperware-packed lunch;
the new recruit, earnest in rolled-up sleeves;
the *True Romance* and thriller readers;
the lazy supervisor trying to command respect.

To work is to pray, but days stretch
long and monotonous as eternity
in my cell, where I toil without hope,
having groped from darkness summoned by bells:
the alarm clock's halo luminous, the plainsong
of birds unbinding, note by note, the night.

Look around this narrow retreat:
you cannot miss my two steel presses,
one seething with memos, the other hoarding forms;
and a cabinet with deckled piles of correspondence
from banks, corporations, accountancy firms.
I am undisputed Lord of the Files.

You can contact me here on weekdays
except during vacations and lunch.
Telephone queries, staff consultations
interrupt this script, as horns, hydraulic sneers,

sirens whimpering like hurt dogs
reach me from the piercing street.

It is not much of a life, serving time,
applying directives or laws,
and therefore not much of a poem,
though revelation strikes occasionally:
a glimmer of wisdom shimmering on my coatstand,
an inkling of transcendence in a momentary hush.

Search my desk with me: stamps and staples,
official envelopes, twine, press cuttings,
address books, antacid tablets, foreign coins.
What was it I set out to find?
A pair of shoelaces? The spare house key?
The secrets of the universe?

Look out across the two small apertures:
you can watch the backs of other blocks,
equal in blandness. One cube of glass
reflects sky, songless birds, slipping sun;
and I can make out clustered heads,
eggs incubating within the metal combs.

Will they ever metamorphose and float away?
Open the window a little before it steams.
Look. Gulls dipping for tea-break crusts
evoke unfrequented shores, skuas, kittiwakes,
wings trimming uneven hems of waves,
chestnut streams charging untamed.

Although I plod routinely on,
greeting familiar faces in the same place,
espying the same familiar strangers in the streets,
changes do occur, marked by collections, whip-rounds.

The amended staff-sheet instructs us to delete
the name of one colleague, killed cycling from work.

As these last words are relayed to you,
my watch's nervous tic advances on half-five.
I exit past the check-in clock where red blobs glow
like tail-lights in the traffic home
or votive lamps we lit as children
praying for a favourable exam result, a steady job.

Office Photograph

for Margaret O'Sullivan

There will be no reunion for this class of people:
some are dead already; one immured in a convent;
others ill, retired, transferred, settled abroad.

But, for the duration of this photograph,
a fresh, foot-stamping morning reigns
(a few wear overcoats) and in the foreground

a wiry tree is barbed with buds.
Behind us, sun disperses shadows
of venetian blinds, like prison bars, on desks

and projects the film of dust specks
fidgeting on our stacked backlog of files.
We stare – clear-eyed, smiling – into a pensionable future.

Dressed in our best and at companionable ease,
we stand oblivious of how such scenes
will flash before us, summoning features

out of memory's frame, blurred by moving time;
and how this tableau, so tranquil in spring light,
so fixed in a known hour and place,

will develop into a focal point of change
as news comes of some name we match, then,
to a placid, frank, unwary face.

Man Going to the Office

(a painting by Fernando Botero)

They all rush to the windows as he leaves.

Wife, child, sister-in-law and servant wave,
though they might also be dismissing him, pushing him away,
wiping him out of their lives with imaginary dusters,
holding palms out for their share of his alms.
Now that his business-suited back is turned, they can relax:
mother pours another coffee, crocheted with cream,
and flicks through glossy magazines, winnowing crumbs of toast;
the open window ideal for sunbathing or keeping track of
    neighbours;
the afternoon free for an unmolested nap, when sister gardens
and the infant's pudgy mouth is hushed with jelly beans.

As he bustles back through the front door at night, muttering,
he will find an immaculate cloth set, a hot meal ready.
After hanging up his bowler crown, dabbing his regal moustache,
he will sit, enthroned, at the head of the rectangular table
permitting the poodle, a foppish courtier, to lick his feet,
throwing it rinds of meat and bread.
And the ladies-in-waiting will pamper him,
bridling their impatience or stifling scorn,
careful not to exasperate him like clients
or provoke, like inefficient secretaries, a fit of spleen.

A Life Study

Here is a woman on a bus
half-way through a book
entitled simply *Life*.

I squint, but cannot decipher
who the author is
or what it is about.

She seems to be enjoying it
or is too absorbed at least
to look out at shoppers

wrapped up in their thoughts.
How is *Life* classified?
Fiction, allegory, myth?

Is she dying to know
the kind of ending it will have?
The book slams unexpectedly.

She gets off at the next stop.

Conception

scum of humanity
seed of pain

multiple warheads
arms racing to stake their claim

the triumphant achieve spina bifida
or ambition malnutrition or fame

and hundreds of millions of sprigs
are disseminated in vain

a lost civilisation
a bedclothes stain

Spoiled Child

my child recedes inside me
and need never puzzle where it came from
or lose a football in the dusty laurel bushes
or sneak change from my jacket to buy sweets

my child will not engage in active military service
or make excuses about its school report
or look up from a picture book, dribbling a pink smile
or qualify for free glasses or school lunch

my child will not become a prodigy of musicianship or crime
and will evince no appetite for hamburgers or drugs
and will suffer neither orgasm nor kidney stones
reduced neither to a statistic nor a sacrifice

my child will not play space games with its cousins
or sit adrift on a grandparent's choppy lap
or slit its wrists or erect a loving headstone on my grave
or store a secret name for frogs or treetops

my child will not be a comfort to my old age
my child will not be cheated or promoted or denied
my child will trail me, like a guardian angel, all my life
its blemishes, its beauty, its shortcomings and promise

forever unsullied and unfulfilled

Day and Night

I

wrapped in a sheer white negligee
      you are a fog-bound landscape
familiar but seen in a new light
      transformed by seamless mist
tantalising, trimmed with tufts of cloud
      I know that after the fog lifts
the climate will turn sultry
      I can detect a sun-like breast
already radiating through the chiffon dawn

II

in hot darkness, the transistor on
      a five-note raga plays
five senses that ascend the scale of longing:
      until the gasps of music peter out
and a taut night is plucked limp
      we are out of meaning's reach
your vellum blotted with invisible ink
      my head at rest
between your breasts' parentheses

Contracts

after Paul Celan

I   *Irisch*

Grant me ingress
to your sleep
to count sheep,
licence to traverse
your dream slopes,
the turbary rights
of your heart's peat,
in perpetuity.

II   *Du Warst*

You were my only loophole
in the repressive act of death:

my last escape clause.

Time-Sharing

In our time together
we are travelling in the heated car,
a violin concerto uncoiling from the radio,
hills streaming with winter cold,
year-end fields worn down to seams,
a blazing quiff of distant dogwood,
burnt meringue of snow on mountain tops.

We blurt past farms and cottages:
those whose era we share
are staring from net curtains
at a morning chill for milking
or for setting off to factories in the town,
their segments of road deserted.
It is like a childhood journey

of sleep and open-eyed surprise,
of hermetically sealed life
in the eternal present
before the final destination is reached.
We hold hands on the gear stick
and, at this moment,
fear for nothing except the future.

Thurles

after Zbigniew Herbert

A childhood too boring for words
is lost without a fragment in that town.
And, so, I have held my tongue about its gutturals;
its sky slated consistently with cloud;
its mossy roofs restraining excesses of rain.

One house watches out for me though.
I know where its colander is kept and the special
knack required to use its tin-opener
and the exact key in which the kitchen door,
scuffed by a ring-board, creaks:

things I cannot depict in dictionary terms,
through heartless words that fail to resonate.
Others are suppressed in embarrassment or pain
(all families have passed their own equivalents
to the Official Secrets Act).

Yet everything there translates into feeling:
the plates the dead have eaten from before us,
the layers of wallpaper that still pattern memory,
the hairline crack in marble that was my fault,
the rose-arched garden explored down to its last stone.

Back in the city, I resort to standard words again.
Unable to identify possessions by their first names,
I call them only by their surnames
– by their brand names –
and will never discover their real names.

Home Affairs

Death is moving into newly-constructed suburbs,
through semi-detached houses, ugly identical twins.
Hired cars will call for widows who have come as brides . . .

Readymix trucks drum up concrete support
where the foundations of our married lives are laid.
We will slice the keyhole loaf of bread together here.

This evening, a rainbow unfolded its colour chart
and I imagined these dwellings once painted, tamed:
the knock of radiators in a dry-lined sitting room;

whispers and bickerings filtered through air vents;
the small-hour lulls only troubled sleepers know
or babysitters waiting for the owners to reach home.

*

Dashed housefronts gleam like popcorn, a mirage
seen from what will be the main road through estates,
bearing working couples, fuel deliveries or crowded bus,
pavements reserved for skateboards, shopping trollies, prams.

We are strolling on its asphalt arc, a desert airstrip
covering ancient cow-tracks, smoothing paths,
a digger's tyre marks – arrowheads – along its verge.
All we will reap from now on in this raw settlement

are plastic piping, gypsum board and brick.
New fridges and washing machines will rust
in mountains of indestructible sediment,
our baths end up as drinking troughs.

*

With a poker for sword, a fireguard for shield,
you provoke the blazing fangs to fume and spit.
Will they know peace who sit quietly in their own rooms?
I trace the braille goosebumps of your body
and begin to lip-read as the night intensifies.

*

It is an ordinary morning without pain.
Sun's spotlight stares from a dishevelled sky,
ruffled with clouds like a safety curtain.
Summer is in heat again: gooseberry scrotums swell,
hard blackberry knuckles will soon ooze with blood.

The window swings out on to a butterfly-light breeze,
a heady aura of sweet peas, rose fumes, poppy seasoning.
Cut lawns exude fresh hay; grasshopper blades whirr;
resinous smells of wood pervade the tool shed.
No bad news breaks today, no urgent summons,

no pacing outside intensive care units.
The sun blossoms in its foliage of cloud
and we fortify ourselves with its light, our house's silence,
against the trouble, bustle, pain
which other mornings will, irrevocably, bring.

FROM

Long Story Short

(1993)

Alchemy

Over many years
I have toiled
to create
Essence of Life
as bath cubes and perfume
on a commercial basis.

But no matter
how much laughter
or even love I add
to the tear ducts and spleen,
I cannot purge
some acrid residues.

To support my children
– who eat everything sweet
they lay their hands on –
I may cut my losses soon
and sell it all off
as an insect repellent

or an anaphrodisiac.

The Death of a Beekeeper

after reading the novel by Lars Gustafsson

Dusk strikes early this far north.
Silver days. Then dark
no house light perforates.

I will not talk of illness.
I will take the dog out walking
to the summer huts

and know I am alive
by the swarms of breath condensing,
tracks left behind me in the snow.

Iced marsh and lake
whichever way I go . . .
I startle elks

a weekender will shoot
when this pale landscape thaws,
gives up its ghost.

Something gnaws my flesh,
like mice behind
a skirting board.

I am a healthy distance
from the hospital,
doctors homing in

on microscopic sections,
masked and gloved,
combing through my cells.

The plaster ceiling
of the sky caves in
and snow cascades,

packs my hut in styrofoam
as though for despatch
(URGENT: PERISHABLE GOODS)

to a more temperate zone.
Soft flakes, white corpuscles,
will ease my pain.

Under Alpine roofs,
the bees are stacked
in viscous sleep,

their sun god hibernates
beneath the frozen lake.
My dog no longer

recognises me by smell;
I am changed.
Snow pollinates the ground,

simplifies the shapes of things.
Then snow blots out
all record of the snow.

Mistaken Identity

Could I begin by asking what you were thinking of as the gunman approached?

Nothing very precise, actually. I was vaguely annoyed at pet owners. It's not fair to those who walk the streets. I'm nearly sure I had a flash of memory also – something reminded me of the nest under the yew at my grandmother's. We found a clutch of warm, fawn eggs one summer there.

A woman, too, I think, a belt tied loosely round her waist?

Yes, that's right. She proved to be a key witness.

I've just recalled the way the hens would tap their legs like tuning forks, then hold their drawling notes long into the afternoon. My grandmother was always making things – knitting or crochet. Or baking. Peach flans, seed cakes, raspberry meringues.

What kind of fear did you experience as the killer was about to strike?

I was a bit behind in my work. A few times in the last month or so a pain had flared down my left thigh. Fear that the eldest would go near the quarry again, that the new video might be robbed during our holiday.

Can you describe how you felt after you learned the news?

It was a kind of reverse dream. You know how when you dream that you've done something with someone (or *to* someone, as it often is) you expect them to remember the experience too. I once flew under the waves with the kids, viewing candy-striped fish from the cockpit . . .

This time, it is they who have the details; I can't remember any of it – the shot, the emulsion of blood, the surgeon, the dizzy lowering into the clay, the statement about mistaken identity.

What would you like one more sight of?

The family, of course. My record rack. A girl in tennis dress. A sky aerated with stars. Swallows in summer that pedal uphill, then freewheel down. A blackbird on my front lawn charming worms. Sparks of moonlight kindling a tree. More ordinary things – the Sunday lunch as it is served, the steaming gold of roast potatoes and chicken skin. The shirts folded after ironing. A running bath.

Any regrets?

That we are as similar in death as life, clustered here under the same headstones. But, to tell the truth, I never wanted to stand out. I would hate to have seen those newspaper reports with my name in them and the neighbours no doubt saying how quiet I was and the bishop praying for my soul and the police confirming I had no subversive connections.

Anything else you miss?

The smell of life given off by the earth that I have no nose for here. Those transparent moments at bedtime nothing had prepared me to expect. The sports results.

Finally, do you forgive your killer?

I accept death as I accepted life – as something to get on with.

3 AM

I'll give him a minute longer
before I break the news.
Another minute of innocence and rest.
He is in the thicket of dreams
he will still be struggling with
as he stirs himself to take my call
wondering who in Christ's name
this could be.
          One more minute, then,
to let him sleep through what
he's just about to wake to.

Way of Life

The longest queues.
The cheapest cuts.

The high season beaches.
The rush hour delays.

The densely populated quarters.
The comprehensive schools.

The public ward for babies.
The public house for celebration.

The special offers.
The soccer turnstiles.

When admission was reduced.
When group rates were available.

During lunchtime or weekend.
During Sunday or bank holiday.

At weddings, parks, parades.
At Christmas markets, January sales.

Wherever people gathered.
When crowds took to the streets.

Fruit Salad

I *Peach*

There's not much point in trying
to cultivate a sultry peach of words.
Just pass me one to stroke, to eat,
or paint it from a glowing palette;
colours dart from apricot to apple,
flames licking velvet hide.
Hold its downy, yielding roundness,
fondle its lightly clothed contours,
taste its golden mean, its sweetness,
before it starts to shrink and shrivel,
starts to wrinkle like a passion fruit.

II *Strawberry*

Strawberries with whipped cream,
a sunset ripple on your plate . . .
A cordate locket, a precious stone;
cut one and expose the marbled core.
The wholesome rubicundity of outdoors,
not the hothouse plastic of tomatoes;
compact, meaty, flecked with seeds,
the bracts a garnish (parsley on beef,
verdant ferns in a bouquet of roses).
A July day provides the ideal accompaniment,
lazy as the cream dripping from the whisk.

III *Pear*

Most easily hurt of fruits,
bruising under a matt coat of skin,
smooth as bath soap inside;
halved, a perfectly stringed lute.

It hangs in a shaft of autumn light
timeless as a bronze cathedral bell
or disturbs the peace and drops
– a hand grenade, pin still intact,
a toppling shell of glycerine.
We take refuge from our troubles in its syrup,
wasps burrowing through heady pulp.

IV   *Apple*

All apples lead back to that first temptation:
trees behind the thatched farmhouse,
forbidden fruit, a warts-and-all beauty,
pupating in pink silk blossom
then fired and glazed in summer,
brushed by a red admiral's wings,
wine-dipped like nectarines or green
as nettles stinging with tart knowledge.
Bite the way back to a primal silence,
your rhythmic crunch shutting out
the world, digesting its hard truths.

V   *Fruit Shop*

Orange skins baked to a crust
(fluffy whiteness underneath);
raspberries like bleeding gums;
melons whose haunches
are tested for ripeness . . .
I buy bananas racked like chops
and apricots, one blemished
with a spot (which I'll slice off,
cheddar flesh wholesome again).
I pinch a bulbous, plum-size grape.
Lemons tumble from an opened crate.

An Uruguayan Bagatelle

on looking into a travel guide

I find it heartening to know
That, should I take flight to Montevideo,
There will be an abundance of hotels,
Salt Atlantic winds, barbecue smells.
If I care to taste the local beef
The variety of cuts will strain belief
And language: no single word like 'steak'
Does justice to the specialities they bake,
Then serve with gravy, rice or mash.
Tips are recommended (use Diners Club or cash).
This guide makes little of the open lands
Rolling from Brazil to coastal sands:
Purple prairies, countless cattle,
Sheep ranches, few Indians (their battles
Bravely lost), big cats decimated.
A beach-loving population, estimated
At three million. Roseate spoonbills on the wing,
Zorzals in the jacaranda sing . . .

Then progress to gambling or whores,
Both legal if pursued indoors.
Teatro Solís nights, the price of gems or leather,
Zum Zum disco club, when to find good weather;
The gaucho statue, parks and shopping streets,
The World Cup stadium (70,000 seats).
But nothing of crime or neighbours' fights,
Idle Sunday pastimes, rural courtship rites,
Of colonels, cloudscapes, office workers' pay,
Tupamaro threats or what the children play.
To check this book, attempt my own rebuttal,
I'd need a PLUNA jet, the airport shuttle.
Its street-map names only those avenues

With tourist promise – I'd quickly lose
My way in anonymous, dull squares:
It is like the pattern of a life, all cares
Blanked out on holiday, the pleasures stressed,
Long plain miles of tedium suppressed.

Taking Life

We live the given life,
follow the gossip of world news,
learn to eat stewed sheep and cows,
tilt the soup-bowl backwards,
use the rear-view mirror
to check impending threats.
Whatever appetites transpire
– boiled sweets, reproduction,
race meetings – we indulge
or sacrifice to God,
our food supply sustained
by charge-card orders
or own-brand bargains
in suburban shopping malls.
We accept the hierarchies
at work, defer to the boss,
moods changeable as climate.
The revelations that occur
are taken more or less on trust,
the flow of menstrual blood,
the red nose blowing cold,
the fear of old age and taxmen,
the deliberations of the bathroom,
having adapted since birth
to illness and disappointment,
growing into the inherited role,
typecast by face and accent,
dressing as convention specifies
to chair a board meeting
or sign on for the dole.

Always within inches of extinction,
we see our lives through
to the bitter end.
Sunday, we read the papers,
mend a daughter's bike;
Monday, sell detergent products
or set the washer to 'long spin'.
We purge ourselves of gloom,
shake off morbid thoughts,
like the eclipsed moon
wiggling free of the stubbly
shadow of the earth,
make the best of things,
enjoy a little fame
– name in the local paper,
championship of darts or golf –
and bring up the children
to be mannerly, adaptable.
This is the life.
There is no mystery about it.
It is what we are living now,
fitting a truck horn to the car
or sitting on a bar-stool
arguing the toss with friends
or amending standing orders
through a show of hands,
our monuments all around us
– churches, prisons, flats,
buildings that scrape
the surface of the skies.

Job

What is it
that my gloomy father
gets so worked up about,
white sheets
rumpled into a lather?

And why is my mother
yielding to his whim?
And why do I
(marked for life)
rush breathlessly to win?

Could they not have turned over
or taken more care
to leave me
in my element,
part of their gulped air?

Residuary Estates

I

After the nausea
of chemotherapy,
after the vomit
and the sores,
bald patients rest
on pillows stuffed
with long hair
from Treblinka,
sleep off
the side-effects
of God and man.

II

Cancerous cells are immortal
laboratory tests suggest.

Is this the everlasting life
my mother now enjoys

that she had prayed for:
the life beyond the grave?

III *After Bertolt Brecht*

wasted by illness
left for dead

flowers rooted
in her soiled body

to weigh so little
she must have taken

enormous pains

      IV

the calm between storms
is the silence in which
the dead are not named
until relatives are informed

Him

I

let me have this pair
of partly-worn shoes
so I can wear them
to the end of the journey
they were intended to complete

I will aim them
where they were meant to go
I will follow in his footsteps
before his tracks are covered over
and his route cut off

II

we bought so much ham
for funeral sandwiches

did we really think
the whole town shared our loss

the surplus meat began to stink
long before our appetites returned

III

the last bar of his soap
became a transparent ghost
and finally slipped my grasp

Body Time

I

They drag you screaming
from the hot bath
of the womb
and dry your spattered hide.

II

The outside world
you enter is less stable.
You must adjust the temperature
with gloves, lovers, smokeless fuel.

III

Now you wallow in a bath
that turns cool – pull the plug
and wait a dreamy minute,
water sloughing like a skin.

IV

And listen to the sound
your life makes
flowing down the waste-pipe,
the stifled noises as it drains away.

Misunderstanding and Muzak

You are in the Super Valu supermarket
expecting to meet me at 6.15.

I am in the Extra Valu supermarket
expecting to meet you at 6.15.

Danny Boy is calling you down special-offer aisles.
Johann Strauss is waltzing me down special-offer aisles.

I weigh mushrooms and broccoli and beans.
You weigh beans and mushrooms and broccoli.

It is 6.45. No sign of you.
It is 6.45. No sign of me.

You may have had a puncture.
I may have been held up at work.

It is 6.55. You may have been murdered.
It is 6.55. I may have been flattened by a truck.

Danny Boy starts crooning all over you again.
Johann Strauss starts dancing all over me again.

Everything that's needed for our Sunday lunch
is heaped up in my trolley, your trolley.

We hope to meet somewhere, to eat it.

Roads Not Taken

How tantalising they are,
those roads you glimpse
from car or train,
bisected by a crest
of grass perhaps,
keeping their
destinations quiet.

You remember a brimming
sea on the horizon
or an arch of trees
in reveries of light;
then a bend that cut
your vision off
abruptly.

Some day you must return
to find out how they end.

In Office

We are marching for work:
people fresh from dream bedrooms,
people whose flesh begins to slip
like old linoleum loosening on a floor,
people with head colds and lovebites,
girls startlingly immaculate,
pores probed with cleanser,
showered hair still wet;
people subordinating their tastes and talents
to the demands of office,
the uniform grind of files.

We forego identity and drive
for the security of such places,
a foyer guard by the spotlit tapestry;
soft furnishings; a constant heat;
gossip with the copier's undulations;
crushes on new recruits; booze-ups
after back-pay from disputes . . .
We are wasting our lives
earning a living, underwriting new life,
grateful at a time of unemployment
to have jobs, hating what we do.

Work is the nightmare from which we yearn to wake,
the slow hours between tea-breaks
vetting claims, scrutinising invoices.
We are the people at the other end
of telephone extensions when you ring,
the ones who put a good face on the firm,
responding to enquiries, parrying complaints,
the ones without the luck to have inherited
long-laned retreats, fixed-income bonds,

who yield to lunchtime temptations,
buy clothes and gadgets, keep retail spending high.

We age in the mirrors of office lavatories,
watch seeds of rain broadcast their flecks
along the screen of tinted glass, a pane
that stands between us and the freedom
which we struggle towards
and will resign ourselves to
when the clock comes round.

Looking Forward

I

We have already advanced
to the stage where we can
convene seminars on cost/yield ratio
and child sexual abuse.
We have reached the point
where genetic engineering can create
a tender, tasty, waste-free sow,
a rindless cut above the rest.
It certainly is not the experts' fault
if minds, like power supplies, break down
under the strain of our pace of life
or if bodies are stifled by the human crush
– tears like oil welling from rock –
or if hunger sears as soils erode:
remember the humblest shanty town
is still the corrugated product
of great skill and ingenuity.
Desert missile tests or rocket launches
may, on rare occasions, prove disastrous;
but we are capable of learning from mistakes
and will get things right the next time.
The alienated are just slow developers,
suffering the growing pains of evolution.
Out of the dung heap of chemical spills,
a thornless mutant rose will sprout,
its scent as fragrant as a new deodorant spray.

II

It's a great age to be alive.
Look at the girls flitting past:
styles were never more enticing,

the denier of nylon never more fine.
And watch the men, so gentle
in their linen suits, their lemon sweaters,
wheeling the baby buggy to a crèche.

Our freedom is unprecedented:
to lose faith in the church,
to choose six lottery numbers and win,
to zoom in close on the adult video,
weather better thanks to global warming
(naked crowds swarming to the beach
turn mole-brown on a sunny spit).

This epoch can accommodate so many tastes:
water skiing, sado-masochism, cottage pie . . .
Lose no time in enjoying earthly goods,
for tomorrow (in a manner of speaking,
at least) we die, although drugs may yet
be found to keep us long-lasting as plastic,
durable as nuclear waste in concrete tombs.

III

The modern order was not guaranteed by basic laws (natural selection, mechanical superiority in anatomical design), or even by lower-level generalities of ecology or evolutionary theory. The modern order is largely a product of contingency.
— STEPHEN JAY GOULD

Chantilly lace and lycra.
Haiku and Norse sagas.
Tow bars and rotary blades.
All here by chance.

False teeth and puncture kits.
Apricot jelly and fax machines.
Laxative pills and Gregorian chant.
All here accidentally.

The stories of your life,
awkward scenes you rescreen
in the bedroom's dark
have no universal moment:

you are on your own
when long-lashed showers,
pebble-dash of hail
hammer on the glass like truth.

Only by eliminating nature,
wiping clean the slate,
will you prove your place
at evolution's peak,

leaving pools of genes
to regroup, a cold
starlit soup on which
a skin begins to form.

Poulaphouca Reservoir

Where ivy grows on a house, the family gets worn out.
– THE POULAPHOUCA SURVEY

1. The name 'Poulaphouca' means the hole of the spirit. Quernstones by the submerged cottages will be ground in the mills of God, fine as the distinction between Father, Son and Holy Spirit.

2. *The Shell Guide to Ireland* calls it 'the great lake of the Liffey hydro-electric works'.

3. Life goes on in that Atlantis. Ivy grows on houses. Haws redden in autumn. Roses are pruned back. Thatch is replenished. Bridal veils float like surf on the clear-skinned water. Turf fires blaze in the lake at sunset.

4. The Field at the Bottom of the Lane is at the bottom of the lake. The Field Under the Well is under water. A school of fish chases in the School House Field. The Coarse Little Field, The Field at the Back of the House, The Inside Field are flooded permanently. Garnaranny, Farnafowluch, Carnasillogue, Coolyemoon are spoken of in bubbles.

5. During summers of drought, you can see outlines of houses. Their owners' names linger at the tip of the lake's tongue. Chimneys poke above the water like the blowholes of hunted whales.

Rose Windows

The road is uphill.
Heathers, ferns.
A mica sheen.
Bracken stirrings, streams.

The train whinnies
into the distance
as you take
a tentative step.

*

Row your boat home
in the sulphurous dusk,
the matt lake lined
with corridors of pine.
Fish rings, shingle,
skidding waves.

*

You wake within range of two cuckoos
– their voices bubbling through algal green –
to find creation has begun:
a blue silk-screen of hills
is printed through a mesh of haze
and everything is new
under the emblazoned sun.

*

An open door admits
the summery smells,
sounds of peaty streams;

hedges blossom with small bells;
thin-sliced, wing-wrapped butterflies
alight on the buddleia bush.

*

The tangerine cottage door,
a colour warm as a hearth fire.
Spring rakes out crocus flames.
A coal-black cat squats
by the frosted window-pane.
A scarf of smoke is tucked
inside the chimney.

*

Gravel heaps
– purpose forgotten –
now host flowers.

Bindweed and nettle
vie for domination.
Ivy scales a telegraph pole.

It's no one's job
to curb
the blackberries.

*

At dusk along
a byroad,
the peppery scent
of tight whitethorn
ephemerally perfect
as you pass

in a collapsing big top
of striped light,
beams streaming
like canal water
through lock gates
of cloud.

*

Strolling beyond the cottage
on your own, breathing peat smoke,
kicking a stone, hayricks
like a tribal village . . .
Row upon row of water glazes strands:
wind-grooved waves stir life
where ochre starfish splay
and lull you with shanty rhythms
to the seabed flickerings of sleep.

*

The last evening, watch
the town lights twinkle
across the bay, like notes
playing a slow air
you might entitle
The Touchstone or The Turning Tide
when you go inside to pack.

*

Squeeze out
all the segments
of this orange day
before it disappears
into the sunset.

Siblings United

for Eithne at 21

Not a care tonight
about which of the family
is out late, sharing the roads
with reckless drivers
or who is short of money,
feeling out of sorts.
We are all here, survivors,
converging at your twenty-first.
You are no longer a child
and I am no longer required
to act as trustee
of our father's will.

United, we declare your independence.
I drink to your health
along with workmates
(you have a full-time job now,
plan a fortnight in France)
or I chat to a slim cousin
remembered with fat legs
propelling a toy scooter,
uncles last seen at a funeral.
We pose for photographs,
slip arms round waists
like life belts . . .

You cut through your name,
dripped in sugar icing
on the home-made cake,
expose the darker
layers underneath.

A close-dancing family
tonight, we celebrate
that you have come of age:
eager, happy, relaxed
in your floral party dress,
showing no after-effects
of your years of grief.

No Man's Land

when the sexes surrender
the weapons of their battle
and step arm in arm
along the precarious peace line
when they lie down together
like lion and lamb
setting enmities aside
for the sake of a natural alliance
        what words soar
        on the warm breeze
        of a whisper
        what mysteries are solved
        what promises waft
        from perfumed rooms
        what loyalties are pledged
        with lace and polished nails
        what treaties are sealed
        by tongues and teeth
        through cindery winter nights
and what pay and prospects
does the future hold
what school-to-shop trajectories of days
what anorak-and-tracksuit routines
walking a neutered dog

Operation

I removed slates
tight as muscle fibre,
opened a flap of skull.
There was a fungal whiff,
sprinklings of wood
like bone dust
on the vascular wires.

Fresh views had not
been aired in this
cramped space for years,
a fine grey matter smeared
the brittle beams,
dotted lines left
signs of worms.

No wonder the roof
had sagged abstractedly:
the house was brain-dead
though its heart
continued to beat
regularly as feet
clambering up the stairs.

Reading Primo Levi on the Train

We breach the ordered peace
of our atrocity-free mornings
forsaking the solitary confinement of sleep
for transportation by commuter train
to where labour pays debts owed
to building society and bank.

We bear food parcels
– salad rolls and fruit –
our working lunches.
A woman cradles a package
– slop bucket or lampshade?
Hair clings to our heads still.
Chains hang from slender necks.
So many of us to kick, to kill,
so much flesh to torture and despise
beneath the modish cuts
of suit and skirt, so many tales
to force abruptly to an end,
so many souls expected home at dusk
to spirit away in cattle trucks . . .

The train clatters on.
Whatever this day holds
we will live to see it through,
march back down gravel drives,
their cindered, osteal sounds,
watch stars like gold-filled teeth
chatter with us in the cold.

Experimental Animals

after Miroslav Holub

It's much cushier when it's raining rabbits
than cats and dogs. The animals for experiment
should not betray too much intelligence.
It grows unnerving to watch their actions mimic yours;
terror and horror you can empathise with.

But, for real heartbreak, take a newborn pig.
Fantastically ugly; possessing nothing
and desiring nothing except its swig of milk;
legs warping under all that weight
of uselessness, stupidity and snout.

When I must kill a piglet, I hesitate a while.
For about five or six seconds.
In the name of all the beauty of the world.
In the name of all the sadness of the world.
'What's keeping you?', someone bursts in then.

Or I burst in on myself.

Arbor Vitae

I

Rooks change
the personalities of trees,
nesting in their brains:

lesions in a winter dawn
as red skies
x-ray nerves and stems.

II

The brain furrowed
with concentration, worry
is starting to unwind.

The hair shaved
for the operation
grows back posthumously.

III

I think of him at times
when my limbs tingle
with pins and needles
then go dead.

Periodical

When I told you I'd seen
a Robert Hass poem called 'Happiness',
you said 'Let's move to wherever
Robert Hass lives.'

Instead, I went back for the magazine
and brought it home to you
as if I believed in happiness
as something money could buy.

The Bottom Line
(1994)

The Bottom Line

[1]

Official standards, building regulations,
fair procedures for dismissing errant staff:
my brain is crammed with transient knowledge
– patent numbers, EC directives, laws.
I pause at traffic lights on the way back
to headquarters; windscreen wipers skim off
visions of this seeping stone-faced town:
a warehouse frontage littered with crates,
lovers locked in an umbrella-domed embrace,
consumers at a bank dispenser drawing cash.
I race the engine, inch the car towards green.

[2]

The kind of suit a man of this age
must wear: single or double-breasted,
turn-ups – or not – on the trousers,
usual lapels; the prescribed space between
the blue stripes of monogrammed shirts . . .
Problems which preoccupy me now, struggling
with pre-meeting notes, will pass away
like fashions: funny collars, ties
my grandchildren can scoff at, looking down
on forebears when, marking some anniversary,
the blanched album does the rounds.

[3]

Quality time at weekends, domestic bliss:
early pathways cordoned off by webs,
I slip out to the shops, return
to bring you tea and newspapers in bed.
On Sundays, every Sunday, I submit to the calm
of supplements, CDs, cooking smells.
All of the mornings of all the weekdays
I leave for work; my office bin fills
with the shredded waste of hours.
A pattern regular as wallpaper or rugs
and no more permanent than their flowers.

[4]

Anxieties you could elevate
to the level of a mid-life crisis
are mere reactions to your dreary days,
the boss's ire, tiresome assignments.
You scan the pink financial pages
on the way home, nodding off and on,
jaded, blinking at suburban nameplates
with each juddering halt the train makes.
Wives are parked by railings; silhouettes
of baby seats; a mumbled greeting, then
you unwind to family anecdotes, TV.

[5]

I am a trustworthy, well-adjusted citizen
at this stage, capable of a commanding
pungency in business talk, good grasp
of office jargon, the skill to rest
phones on my shoulders as I keep tabs,
the ability to clinch a deal convincingly . . .
I recognise a counterpart when our paths
cross in sandwich bar or jazz shop and we nod
to each other with a telling smile, maybe
recall negotiations where we held opposing lines,
all discreet charm now, agendas agreed.

[6]

A life of small disappointments, hardly meriting
asperity or rage, an e-mail cc-ed
to the wrong address, an engagement
missed, a client presentation failing
to persuade: nothing you can't sweat off
at gym or squash. But, in the dark filling
of the night, doubts gather with the rain
which, spreading as predicted from the west,
now leaves its mark on fuscous window panes;
and you wait for apprehensions to dissolve
in the first glimmer of curtain light.

[7]

Pressing tanned flesh, reaching consensus
over some outstanding fact, our well-
scrubbed, nail-filed hands feel soft.
Enough contact with the soil is made
weeding invasive seedlings from the lawn . . .
Best of all, undo the crested tie,
change into fawn slacks and turtle-neck,
white-fringed golfing shoes, commune
with nature between fairway and rough,
taking the air on a bracing Saturday
or sharing honours for the captain's prize.

[8]

When you unclasp your slimline briefcase,
the apple, deep green, high gloss
with waxen sheen, a tea-break snack,
glows among the acetate reports,
symbolising something you can't name
but crave for when your sales, morale
are low – peace, a meaningful existence . . .
You settle for a rental in the west,
family away-days, the company car,
and, who can tell, later you may rise
to a weekend cottage, hens, a bright-red door.

[9]

How did I get this far, become
this worldly-wise, letting off steam
to suppliers, sure of my own ground?
What did my dribbling, toddling stage
prepare me for? What was picked up
from rag books, sticks of coloured chalk,
cute bears, during those gap-toothed years?
So embarrassing the idiocies of my past,
seen from the vantage of tooled-leather
and buffed teak, hands-on management
techniques, line logistics, voice mail.

[10]

At the visitors' car park, the belts
of our trench coats flap with the wind;
we huddle in a confidential group
hoping to have pressed home the point,
a hollow Coke can tinkling on the street.
Then, despite this meeting of minds,
for one long second we run out of things
to say, permit thoughts chill as downturns
to stray into our heads until we contrive
the next move, check watch or schedule,
arrange matters arising, part on a jocose note.

[11]

Photos of my family – wife and sons –
framed in silver near my conference phone
inspire me to seize every chance I get,
make life better for the children
as my parents – sweat of the brow
and all that – did for me; my spouse
is most supportive, clued into the dog-
eat-dog mentality success requires.
Ferrying the kids to school in style
imbues them in the long-term with
some gainful aspirations of their own.

[12]

Pay day, the carefree junior staff
stroll back from the bank, flush with
spending power, indulging in the luxury
of ice-cream, crisps; a PA on maternity,
due to resume soon, parades her baby
like a trophy, weighs with friends
the pros and cons of a career break . . .
It is the wider picture I rake over in my mind:
how gearing can improve; whether to draw
the blind on loss-making subsidiaries
and let the liquidator worry about debts.

[13]

The hidden pain of offices: a mission
statement admonishing me from walls,
the volatility of top brass if sales volume
for a single line falls one per cent.
And customers' righteousness, their touching
faith in the perfectibility of man.
Yet even without the big compensations
– personalised number plates, offshore
tax breaks – I enjoy the hectic pace;
and when, spaced-out, I have an off-day,
I spend my way back to normality.

[14]

All this stuff here I've drudged hard
to own, installed alarms to keep,
could disappear tomorrow at the hands
of some dumb creep in shiny track-suit,
a suede-headed galoot out on bail . . .
Such negative conclusions deprive me
of the full potential of my things,
sailing my boat as often as I should,
shuttering the place for a spontaneous trip –
we give more dinner parties now, invite
boring, trusted friends to look around.

[15]

On the mobile to a client, or passing word
across a dealing room's array of desks,
the way you speak does not brook
disagreement – a patois of mutters and twangs.
Adjusting to home, tense still from
breasting the dense atmosphere of work,
it takes so little to set off a row.
One misplaced phrase and the avalanche
begins: a hail shower of rocks, ropes
failing to grip, your wife as an
ice-maiden throwing glacial looks.

[16]

Reversing into the designated slot
outside your duplex, leaping from
the leather seat of a four-wheel drive,
you feel your life has turned
up trumps; and there are always
further heights to strive for:
set up a consultancy, join the board,
be head-hunted by the rival firm . . .
You are groomed for better things,
well-positioned in promotion stakes,
dogged, uncompromising and still young.

[17]

The peace of Friday evenings after
staff have left the open-plan deserted,
before cleaners key-in for their shift.
Sun flakes out on the carpet, rays
highlight staplers, calculators, pens;
phones flop in cradles: Monday will
inaugurate another week, small talk
over instant coffee; new debenture stock . . .
Meanwhile, suspended between worlds,
I drum on the plastic in-tray, stare down
at the frenzied city, disinclined to budge.

[18]

Women who matter in our lives
– secretaries, wives, one taking on
the other's features in the dark –
adapt their habits to our needs,
shrewd about what should be packed
for the tour of brand distributors,
which calls to allow, how to treat
our moods, our swears: we like our
secretaries efficient, young, breaths
of fresh air, able to laugh off risqué
jokes, remain tight-lipped as wives.

[19]

How much longer will this crystal water
flow, this snow come decked in white,
I wonder, as I pour out bottled spring,
brace myself for questions from the floor
about our new cost-cutting scheme . . .
Even when I mouth defences of our safety
record – latest filters, monitors in place –
I see my children's scornful faces, rivers
shimmering like metal, aluminium-clear,
quivering with farmed fish, squirming with algae,
grey snow lodging on eroded banks . . .

[20]

Before the car ascends the parking ramp
at nine, I drop my working wife off
with a ritual, perfunctory peck.
Tuna salad shared for lunch, a quick
check on appointments – we touch base
if schedules permit, save news of
office manoeuvres for our pillow talk . . .
I glimpse from here the nesting pigeon,
awkward, restless, treading on shells,
then load the spreadsheet's spurt
of ballpark figures, analysing trends.

[21]

In this downward phase of the economic
cycle, I despair of pre-tax growth,
the yield from R & D, lose heart.
Our boardroom's abstract art infuriates me:
dashed-off blobs and squiggles. Trash.
I resent the easy fortunes some make,
smarmy copywriters in white suits,
that painter flogging half-baked wares
for my likes to feel foolish near.
Time again to clear my desk; nothing achieved,
another bitty, gruelling, inconclusive day.

[22]

A torrential morning; drenched to
the cufflinks, I take calls from staff
complaining of sham ailments, voices
straining to sound hoarse or weak . . .
I think back like a parent to their
early promise: none of the we-have-
something-on-you vibes I get now
whenever I insist on strictness. Surely
they wouldn't go so far as to expose me,
trawl files to sniff out iffy deals?
All the things, with hindsight, I regret.

[23]

The nightmare prospect of retirement:
those pathetic cretins condemned to wring
every last comma from the morning paper –
Deaths column to For Sale – sparing
the crossword until later, keeping out
of their wives' hair, put to grass,
to mow lawns, lives devoid of contrast,
an onset of golf-fatigue and gloom,
eager to resume dictating vital memos
to that secretary, the one confidante
they trusted, the one sympathetic ear.

[24]

When the air crackles with threats
– disaffected personnel, final
notices, debts, legal proceedings –
I am lucky to be ex-directory
at home; and I lie low at work,
go aground, invariably *in a meeting*
if I'm pursued – other times, however,
need a high profile approach:
smiling as a football sponsor,
lashing the Budget in a trade mag,
lobbying a Minister for grants.

[25]

Valentine's Day attracts delivery men
cupping rosebud flames that will radiate
on desks through cellophane – no black
spots, no thorns: model of a world
where wars are misunderstandings, hate
is due to childhood traumas and will pass . . .
That people are basically good is agreed
at the canteen tea-break, life as plump
with expectation as the satin card
the postman brings; and love will conquer all
in its glass slipper, right to the final stroke.

[26]

Can a year really have passed since our
last Christmas shindig? Here I am
in the same rut, not a single resolution
carried through, deluding myself that
I'm still in my prime. Yes, it's that
time again: a factitious peace, a ceasefire
between camps, an ambience as sweet
as fake rot on marzipan fruits doled out
from desk to desk; tomorrow's gossip will
concern the boss who'll traipse in late,
suit crumpled, manner untypically mute.

[27]

The unoriginal sins we perpetrate, our guilt
shared like a Christmas bonus: mileage rigged,
spare parts purloined, an office laptop
commandeered to conserve sports club cash,
things troubling when the internal audit
section dreams up dodgy questions;
taxmen, too, the nightmare of close scrutiny
– receipts, excuses, bank statements
to prepare – and the attendant dread
of lay-offs, sackings, three-day weeks,
gaunt, haunting figures begging change.

[28]

Then the time comes when you know
none of your promise will be fulfilled;
the saving roles luck, fame, deliverance
from your job were meant to play . . .
You will slave on till pension day,
eluded by advancement, satisfaction, wealth.
In your head, some plangent melody repeats;
in your mind's eye, a preview of your part
as walk-on stoic, accepting failure in good
heart, battling home against the wind
this night the same as the last.

[29]

Stepping from a lunchtime bistro,
hitting the wet pedestrian-only streets,
I raise the logoed golf umbrella
for a noncommittal client, before we split.
Through the bad reception of rain
come memories of the kissogram French maid
disoriented in a downpour near the admin tower:
satins, bows so much at odds with
our stressed concrete, steel; her dainty
hesitations in the storm, a creature dazed
by headlights who starts turning heel.

[30]

A quite ordinary man, but go-ahead,
the sort you wouldn't throw a second glance
at in the street, let alone comment on.
If you happen to meet him, nothing will
cross your mind unless his smirk
dimly recalls someone you once knew . . .
Though his name won't mean a thing
at present, he is nudging forward, destined
for the top – watch the newsboy hold his
evening paper as he dashes down the steps,
gripping folders, lugging research home.

[31]

The white-cuffed sales rep, guarding
territory, does not add up in the age
of central warehousing; the few we still
keep on are doomed: jaunty, over-groomed men,
sharing jokes and samples at the check-outs,
waiting for a brisk assistant manager
to deign to acknowledge their existence,
counting pallets in a draughty store-room,
raising special offers to eye-level shelves.
Commission in decline, their smiles grow
thin; redundancy will come as no surprise.

[32]

Death, once brushed against,
does not seem in the least
like a stubbly ghost with scythe
reaping dry grass in the graveyard,
but shows up as a brash executive
cutting recklessly across your lane,
lights making eye-contact with yours,
ready to meet head-on as though
by previous appointment; ram home
your car horn like a panic button:
his cellphone's bell will toll for you.

[33]

Phase Two of our unit, I inspect the site
in hard hat and suit, furled plans
like parchment in my hand: a digger's teeth
grind pebble-crunchy, graveyard-yellow clay,
mud choking my oak-coloured semi-brogues.
Faced with such an earth-shattering foray
– the groundwork where progress is rooted –
I sense the desiccated souls of DIY types,
clawing their way through hardware bargains,
prodding at sprockets, widgets, screws,
figuring out some new useless device.

[34]

Guarding against mistakes at any cost,
I steer clear of the PA – lace
blouse and leather skirt – who seemed
ready to reciprocate my interest;
and I try not to fall for lavish gifts
from pushy, new-to-market IT folk
(tokens of appreciation, normal perks
– hampers, country house weekends –
from regulars are perfectly OK): no
rival jerk will do the dirt on me
in first-round interviews for Chief.

[35]

Out on the open road – sun visor, shades,
a guiding hand, the reassuring buoyancy
of tyres; blues and big-band tapes plug gaps
between troubleshooting client operations.
Everywhere seems miles from everywhere,
conflated landscapes scale the heights,
as I check with my secretary by phone
that no shit has hit the HQ fan.
The man at the factory entrance-hut
directs me to the guest zone; I lean
back, grab my linen jacket from its hook.

[36]

Good to hold a stable job in these
recessionary times, friends receiving
letters of regret from the foreign parent,
no golden parachute on offer; yet
tempting just the same to make the break,
venture on a lucrative new challenge.
I scan the vacancies (*self-starter,*
forward-thinking, profit-responsible,
independent but committed to group culture),
conjuring my fate in black and white here,
in terms I can relate to, a dynamic role.

[37]

Scarcely to be acknowledged, even to myself,
days when the very sight of my wall planner
makes me sick, when – instead of tough,
decisive judgements delivered with a quick
peremptory scrawl – I sculpt a paper clip,
chew a ballpoint, gaze at the Alpine calendar.
Suit-coat removed, I scroll through e-mail;
there are press releases to issue, markets
to nail . . . I must switch back to fast track,
delegate; late again tonight, home to my
sleeping child, a wife's taciturn rebuke.

[38]

Over decades, I have said goodbye
to my retiring colleagues, signed
the sentimental cards slyly passed
around, tossed notes into collection
envelopes, stared at grey down fringing
a hand that squeezes mine, conveying
as much emotion as it dares betray . . .
We promise to stay in touch but, of
course, we never do after the hearty
speeches end (tributes, in-jokes from
friends) and they drop out of our cast.

[39]

Walking through the automatic exit,
talking heatedly about the downside
of a greenfield site, I am captivated
by a busker's tune: untainted, pure,
drawn from the rainswept mountainy mind
of an old man counting yearlings in the wind,
the log-shifting silence of his hearth . . .
That music keeps its nerve, unfazed
by the pressing business of the streets;
you continue – 'Right?', 'OK?' – but I,
thread lost, can only mumble and concur.

[40]

First day at the new firm, you treat
warily the insiders you've beaten;
too soon yet to know whose blitheness
camouflages venom. Left to yourself,
taking stock of your plush room, shocked
at the capacious desk-space you must fill,
you speed-read through the introductory
pack (staff pyramids, pie charts, stats)
and worry that – pressures of moving,
children's distress, apart – you may
have misjudged; money isn't everything.

[41]

Like some class of transsexual,
inhabiting the wrong body, you are
trapped in an ungratifying job,
losing self-esteem, but anxious
nonetheless to come plausibly across
as a motivated member of the team;
or is it an out-of-body experience,
so this isn't really you, a goal-
driven executive, setting fresh
parameters, laying down ground rules,
projections tripping off your tongue?

[42]

Creased with the pain of a piercing
duodenal, my thoughts drift to dead
comrades: I pick up from where they
left off, collapsing at a bus stop,
succumbing to a heart attack in bed,
and cut one free of his supportive rope . . .
Each funeral, my resolution was to listen
to staff problems but the real world
does not, alas, allow for much indulgence:
death-in-service pensions are the extent
of my role, lump sums for next-of-kin.

[43]

The flimsiness of steep buildings,
scintillant ice palaces of glass;
sun-spots, structures opposite are
mirrored, warped; filing cabinets,
work stations, rubber plants in tubs
prove amenable to public scrutiny.
It is like walking on air, the sheer
vertiginous layers of stacked light;
lifts surge through molten floors
or plunge to solidities of sculpted bronze,
revolving doors, terrazzo, guards.

[44]

A monumentally awful day, shopfloor staff
baying for your blood; sighs, grumbles,
union officials clamouring for redress . . .
Then the recriminations taking you aback:
like a drowning life, your past is
brandished on the far side of the desk,
your certainty about the fairness
of the way you run the branch is challenged,
old feuds reopen and, with tension high,
you still maintain control, adopt a mild,
sincere tone, just as the books advise.

[45]

A Sunday walk: bees nuzzling perennials,
something stirring under roadside furze.
I seldom find time to take in the view
that cost a hefty premium when I invested
in my prime-location home. I know what
umpteen fishing flies, horse trainers,
software packages – you name it – are called,
but not what this wilderness contains
before planning applications sweep it
all away – motor mowers blazing trails
to a culture of microwaves, antiques.

[46]

Not afraid of risks, not listening to
cagey advice; striking out from time
to time, irrespective of whose toes
you're forced to tread on – whatever's
needed to bring your plans on-stream.
However tight the ship, there will always
be some weak links in line management:
bypass them, oblige the shirkers
to shape up or go – any fallout from your
hardline approach may be made good in
due course; meanwhile, stand your ground.

[47]

All the profitless minutes I expend
on matters not recorded in my timesheet.
The clients' fees (so much per hour
plus VAT) should be reduced to take
account of idle daydreams: hotel trysts
with that ravishing sophisticate
from payroll, sneaking off towards
the border in twin bucket seats . . .
Jolted back from perfumes, limbs
– or thoughts of league scores, injured
props – I continue with put options, liens.

[48]

You could do it in your sleep, the dawn
trek through another empty terminal,
vinyl undergoing a mechanical shine,
gift shops shut – cigars, frilled silk
behind steel grilles – bales of early
papers bursting to blurt out their news . . .
Fanning stale air with your boarding pass,
if you look up from your business–class recliner
during the safety drill, it will be only
to eyeball the stewardess; you itch
to switch your laptop on, rejig the unit price.

[49]

Some networking is necessary to get
to the right people, turning on the charm,
having them eat out of your palm, but never
put entirely on the spot, everything off
the record, a once-only concession you
won't mention to your friends, strictly
between yourselves, without prejudice . . .
Futile dealing with less senior staff,
sticklers for detail, holding progress back.
At clubs, committees, conferences, make a point
of banging heads together, picking brains.

[50]

Sensor lights tested, alarm code set,
I burrow into the high-tog, duckdown duvet;
the number-crunching radio-clock squanders
digital minutes like there was no tomorrow.
Who will remember my achievements when
age censors me from headed notepaper?
Sometimes, if I try to pray, it is with
dead colleagues that I find myself communing . . .
At the end of the day, for my successors too,
what will cost sleep are market forces, vagaries
of share price, p/e ratio, the bottom line.

FROM

Quality Time

(1997)

You

Be yourself: show your flyblown eyes
to the world, give no cause for concern,
wash the paunchy body whose means
you live within, suffer the illnesses
that are your prerogative alone –

the prognosis relates to nobody but you;
you it is who gets up every morning
in your skin, you who chews your dinner
with your mercury-filled teeth, gaining
garlic breath or weight, you dreading,

you hoping, you regretting, you interloping.
The earth has squeezed you in, found you space;
any loss of face you feel is solely yours –
you with the same old daily moods, debts,
intuitions, food fads, pet hates, Achilles' heels.

You carry on as best you can the task of being,
whole-time, you; you in wake and you in dream,
at all hours, weekly, monthly, yearly, life,
full of yourself as a tallow candle is of fat,
wallowing in self-denial, self-esteem.

Selling Out

I

We contracted to sell the lot.
The angle of attack of heavy rain.
The bedroom with the rising damp spot.
The dawn shunt of a gypsum train.
The night creak of boards, metallic pings.
The tree fungi like heaped-up plates.
The valedictory spider tying strings.
Swivel press. Clothesline. Blackbirds in spate.

II

When the sparrow tilted the balance of the pear tree.
When the apples were setting out their stalls.
When the scaly sea sparkled like a fizzy drink.
When the yew thirsted for the juices of the moon.
When your lavender deck chair sprawled
near the gangly hollyhocks.
When the palm tree – so alienated all winter –
fanned itself against premeditated heat.
When the robin came within two feet of your wellingtons.
When the neighbours were away.
When stamens bowed with gold dust.
When rust had yet to blight the lilacs.
When the white of the indecisive butterfly
was like the surface on a bowl of double cream.
When you returned upstairs
and stole a last glance at the view.
When you found the sky had misted over.
When the deed was done.

Customs

A small airport. A plane
lost in a fog of thought
  like a train nettle-deep
  in a siding. It has seen
mountain tops streaked with zebra
skins of snow, fields like cracks
  on an Old Master landscape,
  flickering cities – buried
treasure – through snagged clouds.

Early arrivals delayed,
the girl at the Hertz desk
  jokes with the passport clerk.
  A cleaner leans on his mop.
And the control tower
rising from the mist
  like a border look-out
  sets the Customs official
on a reverie of his own,

when the weight of January snow
buckled the roof on his
  solitary outpost; kicking stones
  along the byroad in July
– a tractor armed to cut hay
would bring a moment of diversion:
  as that engine dwindled, the stream
  could be heard more clearly,
the grass growing under his feet.

Water

The miracle of water
is that it tastes of nothing,
neither of chlorine nor peat,
not of old tap fittings or dead sheep.

Water was the first mirror,
drinking images of beauty,
showing their wrinkled future
in the mildest breeze.

Water clings to its neutrality,
changes state at boiling point,
finds the level at which
tensions cool, limbs relax.

It is the splinter of ice in the heart,
the white blood of the snowman,
the burst main flooding
from Christ's frozen side.

Sun Spots

A hazy dawning.
The jogger's trainers
stained by dewy grass.

Insects mix and mingle.
Morning clears its throat
through a cock's crow.

A horse grows from sleep
to full height,
kick-starts into life.

I shut out the news,
gag the car stereo's mouth
with a Purcell ode.

And sun triumphs in the end
– resplendent, brassy, baroque –
trumpeting the day.

                *

Autumn falters to a cube
of tawny light, a stage
where Chekhov is performed.

By now, the lavish
evenings of midsummer
have been squandered.

Isobars tighten like layers of clothes.
The year is an off-season dacha,
ready for boarding-up,

a play in which a band
is made out in the distance,
marching away. Wafting. Fading.

*And time will pass
and we shall be forgotten:
our faces, our voices, our pain.*

*

The momentary glint of tin,
the flash in the pan,
has remained precious this long,

long enough for the still life
painter's name to be unknown,
wiped out like flesh and bone,

like the bruised fruits
(liver plums, skull pears)
the viewers stalk

with hungry eyes,
ripe for the simple truths
the sun bares,

making light of water,
pinpointing
the pitcher's soul.

Pioneers

for Olga Kelly and Tom Sheedy

How did we stand it?
Our squat bungalows plonked down
in the middle of a muddy field,
unfinished and unadorned.

Everything was unprecedented, strange,
edged with an expectant silence.
Pick and spade to hand, I manfully
staked my pride on an undulating lawn . . .

The house was ours; ours the pressured
water snarling from its taps; ours
the otherworldly quiet of its attic ribcage,
neat and insulated as a chaffinch nest.

Light fell gently on us sometimes,
gasping at the beauty of a morning glass
of orange juice, scooping a chute of sun
that dusted our sparse furniture with warmth,

finding its way to dew-sprayed lettuce
left by our good neighbours on the sill.
Next to the rubbish infill at the roundabout,
the precast concrete of the industrial estate:

forklifts, containers, CCTVs, plywood crates,
slavering guard dogs; wildflowers swept
clay ramparts under lumpy yellow carpets.
Environs so Iron Curtain, so consigned

to squalor, shoddiness and grot,
that when our poet-friend had finally
identified our nameless street,
Hello there, Comrades was his opening shot.

The Next Poem

My next poem is quite short and it's about something most of you will recognise. It came out of an experience I had on holidays a couple of years ago. In fact, I'm pretty sure I'm correct in saying that it's the only poem I've ever managed to write during my holidays, if you could have called this a holiday – it bore all the hallmarks of an endurance test.

There's a reference in the poem to roller canaries, which become more or less mythical birds in the last line. I hope the context will make that clear. Incidentally, this poem has gone down extremely well in Swedish translation – which maybe reveals a bit about *me*! A word I'd better gloss is 'schizont'; if I can locate the slip of paper, I'll give you the dictionary definition. Yes, here we are: 'a cell formed from a trophozoite during the asexual stage of the life cycle of protozoans of the class *Sporozoa*'.

OK then, I'll read this and just two or three further sequences before I finish. By the way, I should perhaps explain that the title is in quotations. It's something I discovered in a book on early mosaics; I wanted to get across the idea of diversity and yet unity at the same time, especially with an oriental, as it were, orientation. And I need hardly tell this audience which of my fellow-poets is alluded to in the phrase 'dainty mountaineer' in the second section. Anyway, here it is. Oh, I nearly forgot to mention that the repetition of the word 'nowy' is deliberate. As I said, it's quite short. And you have to picture it set out on the page as five sonnet-length trapezoids. Here's the poem.

Faith, Hope, Loss

1. I stumble on you, prostrate by the door, flat out in a frenzied search for a dropped ear-ring or stone, as if vowing to reform your life in exchange for the recovery of the trinket.

2. With mounting helplessness and rage, my route is retraced in my mind, until I suspect it was in the airport phone booth that I left the missing bag.

3. Losing a loved one. Seeing a daughter eviscerated by cancer, her kindly discoloured face beneath the numbered hairs.

4. To be one of the world's 5.7 billion people: reaching climax, anaesthetised with blockbusters and booze, delving in bins for found art, discarded food. Or one of the three unique species annihilated every hour as grasslands, open-cast mines, weekend shacks impinge.

5. The ditch of lisping water laced with greens, awash with swaying tendrils, dunked leaves, is cemented over; spring light of primroses extinguished; slashed briars where a robin summed up April dusks.

6. Bliss consists of the smallest things. The bus already there to meet the all-night train. Unhappiness lies in what we miss.

7. You are on your knees, convinced that what seems irredeemably lost continues to exist, keeping faith that – given time and patience – it will be restored.

Variations for Wind

*When a wind like this is blowing, it somehow comes home to you
that man has been* flung *into the world.*

— ANDREI SINYAVSKY

I

Forget the gentle zephyr of legend,
the washday breeze dislodging suds

like cherry blossom from the line,
the therapeutic music of wind

at a bellows-driven, pine-crackling fire . . .
Whipped up by a cloud-furrowed

brooding sky, gusts lick the caves
like flame, swig from window glass:

a hurricane crescendo drowning
naked cries, a day of judgement

as you rise from sleep to Gods
whom neither winds nor seas obey.

II

Think in terms of hiding
as storms hit their winter stride.

Raw wind gnaws your bones;
turn the other cheek,

turn from the foam-streaked sea
to the haven of the pub.

Knock back a hot whiskey,
discard the sopping anorak.

Keep your eyes peeled
for anyone in the room you know.

Through a headstrong plume
of cigarettes, begin counting days.

III

Sang-froid. The way the bird
would tune up every dawn.

Something set it going
like a car alarm; all through

atonal January, the strident
woodwind of the gales,

it tried to stave off harm
as though by scaling high notes

it could stop the flexing
cypress limbs it perched on

from toppling down upon us
in the next aggressive gust.

IV

You must leave – today, not tomorrow –
the face behind the ticket kiosk

seems to say. It's an ill wind
that blows: if not a Venetian sirocco,

the plutonium breeze ripping
through bilge-thickened seas,

a *force majeure* throwing spores
of incaution to the winds.

The sewage boat discharges
filmy cargo, like crude oil,

off beaches where Tadzios paddled
in gold stoneground sand.

      V

That we will come,
ultimately, to nothing

– this the wind ensures,
threatening to break and enter,

belching black fumes of cloud
around the rheum–eyed moon;

and you start to understand,
looking out at where umbrellas

struggle like the bony wings
of prehistoric birds,

this planet is not habitable;
streets are paved with silver rain.

VI

Yes, we do have homes to go to
when the nights are cold and drab,

places we can be ourselves in,
universal potholed streets

along which someone scurries
through the shadows always,

the inlaid gem of a cigarette
above his leather jacket, jeans.

You sink into the fireside chair
that has assumed your very contours,

outstare the flames of coal a wind
is taunting, buff your muddy shoes.

VII

A churning, stomach-turning,
seasick sea: a gothic scene

as, once again, rain clouds –
ragged curtains – lacerate the moon.

Waves gasp ashore, collapse,
unload their concave burdens

and, sieved through shingle,
pour off surplus water on dry land,

rub salt into the wounded air.
Seas somewhere harbour

warmer colours, weathered copper
melding into verdigris. Azure.

VIII

After winter, like a chronic illness,
has kept up its tired routine,

the analeptic light which you
aspire to will strike soon

out of the blue: creepers stir
from purdah, decked with

festive blooms, butterflies
rise like the jubilant flags

of a liberated archipelago,
yellow flowers baste tall grass.

You recall how wild the roses smell
when doused by summer showers . . .

All

all journeying together
the living and the dead
all that are alive
all that will be dead
all that will be born
all that ever lived
remains accompany us
like meteorites
husks of dead bees
tusks of dead elephants
mandibles of termites
snouts of seahorses
spouts of whales
necks of giraffes
not a speck of moth's
dust is mislaid
wings of bluebottles
stings of scorpions
suction pads of leeches
gill chambers of fish
species certified
extinct on shale
still dwell among us
as alive once
as the neighbours
of our own future graves
who pass us daily
on the teeming streets

Sin

grant us sin, O Lord
we need to believe in sin
in the halo of pain

yielded by wealed buttocks
the body and blood savoured
in the beads of sudden jism

we need to believe it is wrong
to anoint each other with our chrism
as if lives depended on this

we need to believe it is wicked
to eavesdrop at the peak-hour rate
on cheap recordings of bored wives

do not forgive us, O Lord
our sense of emptiness after the event
our hollow cries of pleasure, woe

spice with a heightened shame
the slow ritual of removing vestments
the awe with which hands tremble

in the presence of transient flesh
that even to the naked eye
is Your own image and likeness

teach us to treat sweet secret passages
as dens of iniquity and filth
when, guilty and abashed,

we turn back to Your clasp

Time Check

To tell the hour, you need
an old-style wind-up wall-clock
swinging the lead of its pendulum,
marching in time with the seconds,
a child keeping step with a parade;

the sound of time when – too engrossed
to notice – we let it pass us by
or when it punctuates the silence
a lovers' tiff fomented, each moment
a drip of Chinese water-torture.

In the aftermath of a death,
the pendulum is stilled: a heart
snatched in a coroner's gloved hand;
released later, a pulsating fish,
the flicked blades of its fins

slicing through shaded streams.
Time must be heard no less than seen
as it goes around in circles.
A girl anticipates her first menses,
her harassed mother her last;

a dog barks from a distant farm
all through the vigil of a sleepless night . . .
The clock rations out your seconds,
checks them off, tots them up aloud.
Then its trance-inducing pendulum asks

for your childhood back, your life.

Talking Shop

What does it profit a man to own the poky
grocery shop he sleeps above, unlocking at eight,
not stopping until some staggeringly late hour?

Even before opening, he has driven his van
to the market, replenished supplies of bananas,
apples – nothing too exotic for local demand.

Seven days, he takes his place behind formica,
the delights of his mother's age preserved
in shelves of jelly, custard, sago pudding.

Peaches on his waterlogged display outside
will still be smarting from the previous day's
rain as though steeped in their own juice,

cabbage-leaves prismatic with drops.
A propped radio brings up-to-the-minute news
or, in slack periods, he reviews things

at first-hand, standing sentry in the doorway,
watching nobody come or go from the plain-
faced cottages opposite: once they unleashed

mid-morning shoppers; now wives work,
supermarkets supply all but a few spontaneous
needs: shoelaces, low-fat milk, shampoo.

Finally, having wound the shutter down again,
the life he leads is his business exclusively.
Perpetual light shines on the tiny cash box.

You will see for yourself, through the slats,
the rows of cans like tin hats, suits of armour,
maybe hoarded as a foretaste of impending war.

Success Story

Your name is made.
You have turned the company around,
downsized franchise operations,
increased market penetration
on the leisure side,
returned the focus to core business.
Man of the Month in the export journal,
ruffler of feathers, raiser of dust,
at the height of your abilities.

You don't suspect it yet, but things
are destined to go gradually downhill.
This year or the next you will
barely notice any change – your tan offsets
the thinning of your blow-dried hair,
you recharge your batteries
with longer weekend snooze-ins,
treat back trouble with heat pad and massage,
install an ergonomic chair for daytime comfort.

Behind closed boardroom doors
there will be talk: not quite
the man you were, losing your grip,
ideas a bit blah, in danger
of becoming a spent force.

The prospect of an early
severance package will be tested
delicately over coffee, low-key as
'Can you pass the sugar, please?'

The flamboyant young blood you trained
will start talking down, interrupting
half-way through your report
on grasping brassplate opportunities.
You will hear yourself say *In my day*
more often than you should.
Bite your tongue.
Brighten your tie.
Show your old readiness to fight.

Them and You

They wait for the bus.
You spray them with puddles.

They queue for curry and chips.
You phone an order for delivery.

They place themselves under the protection
of the Marian Grotto at the front of their estate.

You put your trust in gilts, managed funds,
income continuation plans.

They look weathered.
You look tanned.

They knock back pints.
You cultivate a taste for vintage wines.

They get drunk.
You get pleasantly inebriated.

Their wives have straw hair.
Yours is blonde.

They are missing one football card
to complete the full set.

You keep an eye out for a matching
Louis XV-style walnut hall table.

They are hoping for a start with a builder.
You play your part in the family firm.

They use loose change, welfare coupons.
You tap your credit card impatiently on the counter.

They lean over the breeze-block wall to gossip.
You put down motions for the Residents' AGM.

They have a hot tip for Newmarket.
You have the inside track on a rights issue.

They go over the top.
You reach it.

They preach better pay.
You practise it.

Voyager

I

He will live a little longer: sadness taints
the air like gas, a vapour of doleful music
escaping the radio's capsule; death signs
clarify like stars that filled his vision one night
on a river as eyes adapted to the dark,
heat lightning launched distress flares.

II

The boating holiday we'd planned to treat
him to: sedge and reed-beds; willows trailing
slender arms in water, as if from a skiff;
calm evenings with reading light till ten
when mayflies tantalise the slurping lake,
sun comes filtered through a sieve of leaves.

III

Rocks, lock gates, whirlpools, tidal flows:
his fingers trace the mapped obstacles faced
between the river's origin and the cold,
salt-preserved finality of sea; cut water
healing in his wake, he rows, as though
for dear life, towards the beating sun.

Home

when all is said and done
what counts is having someone
you can phone at five to ask

for the immersion heater
to be switched to 'bath'
and the pizza taken from the deepfreeze

FROM

Weather Permitting

(1999)

Either

They are somewhere in the world, pouring soya milk
on porridge during the dream-time before work,
     or sprouting thick fungal whiskers
     in a graveyard's penetrating damp –
the ones I used to know, with whom I lost
touch, who were once the mainstay of my
     gossip: squash partners, office colleagues,
     obnoxious neighbours, friends of friends.

As I speak, they scrutinise the milk carton's text
or subside more comfortably into the sleep
     that resurrection's long-haul wait entails.
     Our paths crossed, then grassed over again.
They are either alive and well or decomposing
slowly in a shroud; I could either call them up
     and chat, or confirm that they are ex-directory now.
     It is a matter of life or death.

Background Music

It is not music you are listening to, it is not
your song they are playing, but the time outdoors
those same chords struck: Mahler's hammer blows fell
as dusk crashed down like cymbals on the perspex
shell where the orchestra was pitted against
birdsong, the sky's membrane raised like a roof.

It is not the melody but the warm air it drifts on,
through a window open to let paint dry, a daughter
prying the piano keys for notes in the dull acoustics
of an immaculate white room; or a string quartet silhouetted
before a curving bay: you have travelled east into a second
spring, rays cascading through an ice-melt of blue glass.

And that pop-song: ignore the ear-rotting, saccharine words;
let it transport you back to school holidays, cycling
torpid afternoons away, circling the oblong square.
Stuccoed houses in a Mitteleuropa city, a Sunday heavy
with dust of ribboned war wreaths, history; dark-eyed surveillance
from backstreet bars, a gypsy guitar wafting like nicotine.

A bugler's reveille from his campsite, dissipating river mist.
An organ fugue through incense after a cathedral Mass
at which the host clung to the cupola of your mouth.
Scratchy childhood tunes, loudhailed by a carnival, croon
through bloated heat; you try to sleep amid the corncrake-hoarse
excitement – cross-hatched sounds that fuse in memory now,

a Charles Ives symphony improvised on the spot.

The Celtic Tiger

Ireland's boom is in full swing.
Rows of numbers, set in a cloudless blue
computer background, prove the point.

Executives lop miles off journeys
since the ring-roads opened, one hand
free to dial a client on the mobile.

Outside new antique pubs, young consultants
– well-toned women, gel-slick men –
drain long-necked bottles of imported beer.

Lip-glossed cigarettes are poised
at coy angles, a black bra strap
slides strategically from a Rocha top.

Talk of tax-exempted town-house lettings
is muffled by rap music blasted
from a passing four-wheel drive.

The old live on, wait out their stay
of execution in small granny flats,
thrifty thin-lipped men, grim pious wives . . .

Sudden as an impulse holiday, the wind
has changed direction, strewing a whiff
of barbecue fuel across summer lawns.

Tonight, the babe on short-term
contract from the German parent
will partner you at the sponsors' concert.

Time now, however, for the lunch-break
orders to be faxed. Make yours hummus
on black olive bread. An Evian.

Jet Age

Years, centuries, millennia will pass. Highways and airports will be
reclaimed by twitch grass or covered with sand.
— IVAN KLÍMA

The stories we will regale our grandchildren with,
aluminium whales plunging to within inches of our lives,
diving down on cities, capsules stacked above the tarmac
before wheezing to a breathless halt (where swaying grass
will replace windsocks, fuel-trucks rust on apron cracks).

Spread-eagled tonnage taking off, a magic carpet rising
on its dust, vapour trails like silver rails to glide along,
live cargo strapped to padded seats commanding sight of land
stranded in sea-water; clouds like rose-tipped corries,
exhausted quarries, frozen canyons, unconquered peaks . . .

So inured to mystery were our people, we will say,
they took for granted sprayed glitter of night cities,
towns riveted to the ground, but stirred from newspaper
or snooze to adjust their watches and their headrests,
choose capriciously among the complimentary liqueurs.

Nor

'There didn't have to be 2,000 diseases
of the skin', I remember someone commenting.
Nor 17,293 painfully slow routes through the vomitory
before being thrown to the lions of death.
Nor 11,416 ways of feeling wounded.
Nor 89,010 gradations of loneliness
calibrated on traffic islands, country lanes.
Nor 29,109,352 reasons to toss and turn at night.
Nor stage fright, nor honeymoon cystitis.
Nor *esprit de l'escalier*, nor so many calories in cream.
Nor sexually transmitted fatalities, nor smoker's cough.
Nor 250,000,000 tons (live weight) of humanity
to experience these things, nor however many
newborn pounds were dragged screaming, added
to the tally, since my opening line.

In Memory of Alois Alzheimer
(1864–1915)

I

Before this page fades from memory,
spare a thought for Alois Alzheimer,
called to mind each time

someone becomes forgetful,
disintegration vindicating
his good name.

II

His is the last image assigned
to the ex-President who has slipped
from public view; soiled sheets
give credence to his thesis;

his territory is marked out
by the track of urine
dribbled along the corridor
of the day-care centre.

III

Lie closer to me in the dry sheets
while I can still tell who you are.

Let me declare how much I love you
before our bed is sorely tested.

Love me with drooling toxins, with carbon monoxide,
with rope, with arrows through my heart.

Snail's Pace

I look down on the snail as on a container ship
seen from a plane, its slow pace an illusion
caused by distance, filigree silver wash a ruff
of sea spray. It is on its way, no doubt, to feed
off my garden, cold mucous mouth watering at the thought
of a sweet-and-sour meal of compost, leaves.

I raise a foot, needing to hear a shell's crunch,
a squelch against cement. Or I might nip inside
for salt to liquidate it, watch the textured stretch-
fabric flesh fizz into extinction; no one is sentimental
towards snails, oozing as though squeezed from rusty tubes.
Yet I let this specimen pursue its sluggish routines in the end.

The horns scout like a ship's antennae, ready
to warn but pointless when faced with aerial attacks.
I even know the damp ivy-clad segment of the back wall
where it skulks on dry days, lurking in its chestnut shell,
sticky with phlegmatic glue; and though sometimes I reach over,
prise it off to teach it who is boss, I can never quite rise

to the callousness required to play God with its life.

Votive Candles

Burning candles toast
a corner of the church:

To your good health,
happiness, success . . .

One lighting the next
like a nervous

chain smoker's cigarette:
little rockets, boosters,

launched to heaven,
knuckle-white with pleading.

When they gutter,
stutter, dwindle, taper off,

what is left
of inflamed hopes

is a hard waxen mass,
a host;

the shard of soap
with which

God washes
His spotless hands.

A Station

after Jenő Dsida

An official announcement crackling like deep-fried fat
that our branch-line train would be three hours delayed.
A garbled explanation, some reference to points failure.

And so this Thursday night, I stamp feet on the platform's pier,
venturing to the edge of choppy dark, like a man walking a plank.
Back in the yellow, dank, retch-smelling station building,

I read maps cracked on walls, see pierced hearts squeezed
in felt-tip between names; a revving engine raises,
dashes hopes, abandoning me to loneliness again, a pattern

repeating like the taste of supper in my mouth, thoughts
of betrayal in my mind. The blood is faltering in my veins.
A pale man, slumped near the blinded ticket kiosk, eyes

the clock; a young woman, tightening her veil of silence,
looks aside – it would be good to hear companionable sounds.
No chance. I listen as my inner demons prophecy what cruxes

lie in wait. Telegraph scaffolds line embankments.
Peter could snooze until cock-crow. James drools into
the neat pillow he has made of his scarf. John,

sleeping rough on concrete, keeps watch on his bad dreams.
Restless, I resume my platform vigil, fear streaming down
my forehead in the signal light's unyielding red.

Then, like switching tracks, I start to pray that my train
might never arrive, that my journey be indefinitely delayed,
forward connections missed, that my cup might pass from me.

Tomorrow

I

Tomorrow I will start to be happy.
The morning will light up like a celebratory cigar.
Sunbeams sprawling on the lawn will set
dew sparkling like a cut-glass tumbler of champagne.
Today will end the worst phase of my life.

I will put my shapeless days behind me,
fencing off the past, as a golden rind
of sand parts slipshod sea from solid land.
It is tomorrow I want to look back on, not today.
Tomorrow I start to be happy; today is almost yesterday.

II

Australia, how wise you are to get the day
over and done with first, out of the way.
You have eaten the fruit of knowledge, while
we are dithering about which main course to choose.
How liberated you must feel, how free from doubt:

the rise and fall of stocks, today's closing prices
are revealed to you before our speculating has begun.
Australia, you can gather in your accident statistics
like a harvest while our roads still have hours to kill.
When we are in the dark, you have sagely seen the light.

III

Cagily, presumptuously, I dare to write 2018.
A date without character or tone. 2018.
A year without interest rates or mean daily temperature.
Its hit songs have yet to be written, its new-year
babies yet to be induced, its truces to be signed.

Much too far off for prophecy, though one hazards
a tentative guess – a so-so year most likely,
vague in retrospect, fizzling out with the usual
end-of-season sales; everything slashed:
your last chance to salvage something of its style.

Hay Barn

Riches of hay, hoarded
away in the barn, a cache
stuffed under a mattress,

were withdrawn over
winter, wads forked out
from a frosty cart.

Loose clumps
poked from smoking
mouths of cattle

who itched long
alligator chins
on wattle posts.

Though ransacked,
whittled down,
the hay smelt yet

of dusty summer,
of the beehive domes
swept dreamily home

on a horse–drawn float,
listing, hem brushing
against the uneven field,

sides ripping on thorns,
losing wisps to
a hedge–congested lane;

then unclasped, uncorseted
from twine bindings,
added to the stockpile

with sweaty, shirtless heaves
of men relieved
to have crammed each cavity

before the rodent-patter
of rain, creating a sanctuary
again, love nest,

escape hatch
for brooding hens
with dung-speckled eggs.

Ruminate on abundance
there some Sunday
after Mass,

still in your suit,
rooted to the ground
with awe.

Towards a Cesare Pavese Title

(Verrà la Morte e Avrà i Tuoi Occhi)

Death will come and it will wear your eyes.

Death demands the handover of your eyes.

Death eyes you, stares you in the face.

Then death assumes the running of your eyes.

Death powders cheeks, shadows eyes.

Death would take the eyes out of your head.

Death will seize your assets, cut off your eye supply.

Death lashes out at your defenceless eyes.

You are up to your eyes in death.

Death takes after you, eyes the image of yours.

You would recognise death with your eyes shut.

Death will give you dagger glances, evil eyes.

Death makes eye contact at last.

Death will come and it will steal your looks.

9 AM

A metal clatter of shutters.
A shattering of the street's silence.
A turning of keys, an unbolting of doors.
A reversing of 'CLOSED' verdicts.
A striped sun-awning is goaded
from its lair by a long pole.
Mobile signs are placed strategically
on the pavement, the direction of arrows checked.
Blue security men, not yet on their guard,
step out for a smoke or breathe the light.
The gift boutique smells of buffed wax polish,
the cosmetics section atomises into perfumes.
Brasso revamps an estate agent's image.
Two tramps, disturbed in doorways, fold up blankets.
Jewellers unlock their strongroom stock of gold rings
and bracelets, slip them back into plush velvet displays.
Name-tagged assistants drip bagged coins into tills.
Flowers, bleary-eyed from all-night truck journeys,
revive in cool vases, open wide.
Dust is taken in by vacuum cleaners
or brushed aside, swept towards gutters.
A hairdresser assesses a fringe
of tepid water with her hand.
'The usual' for a bakery customer means
a roll and butter, a tea-break muffin.
Bacon, egg, sausage in a coffee shop.
A newspaper, a slice of toast.
9 o'clock and all goes well.
Everyone is present and correct.

Friday

We are driving home.
Work is over, the weekend ours
    like a gift voucher
to spend as we feel inclined.

    We pass the armed guard
of whitethorn, the guard
    of honour of poplars,
until our favourite

    half-mile stretch
where a canopy of branches
    spans the road
like a triumphal arch.

    Our car tunnels into
this leafy underpass,
    entering its funnel,
its decompression chamber.

    Sheep are shearing fields;
lambs bound like woolly dogs
    just released from the leash.
We have squeezed through

    the filter of trees
and now, renewed, detoxified,
    we are on the downward
slope towards home.

Only

It is only skin.
It can be artificially cultured these days.

It is only breath.
As often sour as sweet.

It is only nerve tips.
Invariably sensational in response.

It is only lips, one on top of the other.
Shedding their unsavoury scales.

It is only warmth.
Everyone hovers around the 37° mark.

It is only hormones, emitting primitive signals.
Easily reproduced under laboratory conditions.

It is only blood.
The dilation can be clinically explained.

It is only desire.
An impulse inspired electrochemically.

It is only a fluttering heart.
It has a finite number of strikes.

It is only one organism among many.
A million clones could be arranged.

It is only that your moment has arrived.
It is only for now.

To a Love Poet

I

Fortysomething did you say? Or more?
By now, no one could care less either way.
When you swoop into a room, no heads turn,
no cheeks burn, no knowing glances are exchanged,

no eye contact is made. You are no longer
a meaningful contender in the passion stakes.
But a love poet must somehow make love,
if only to language, fondling its contours,

dressing it in slinky tropes, caressing
its letters with the tongue, glimpsing it darkly
as though through a crackling black stocking
or diaphanous blouse, arousing its interest,

varying the rhythm, playing speech against
stanza like leather against skin, stroking words
wistfully, chatting them up, curling fingers
around the long flowing tresses of sentences.

II

Never again, though, will a living Muse
choose you from the crowd in some romantic city –
Paris, Prague – singling you out, her pouting lips
a fountain where you resuscitate your art.

Not with you in view will she hold court to her mirror,
matching this halter-neck with that skirt, changing her mind,
testing other options, hovering between a cashmere
and velvet combination or plain t-shirt and jeans,

watching the clock, listening for the intercom or phone.
Not for your eyes her foam bath, hot wax, hook-snapped lace,
her face creams, moisturisers, streaks and highlights.
Not for your ears the excited shriek of her zip.

Look to the dictionary as a sex manual.
Tease beauty's features into words that will assuage
the pain, converting you – in this hour of need –
to someone slim and lithe and young and eligible for love again.

Life Cycle

in memory of George Mackay Brown

January. Wind bellows. Stars hiss like smithy sparks.
The moon a snowball frozen in mid-flight.
George is rocking on his fireside chair.

February. The sea loud at the end of the street.
Ferries cancelled. Snowdrops seep through dampness.
George is sitting down to mutton broth.

March. Oystercatcher piping. Early tattie planting.
Gull-protected fishing boats wary of the equinoctial gales.
George is tired by now of his captivity.

April. Cloud boulders roll back from the Easter sun.
The tinker horse, a cuckoo, in the farmer's field.
George is taking the spring air on Brinkie's Brae.

May. Scissors-tailed swallows cut the tape, declare summer open.
A stray daddy-long-legs, unsteady on its feet as a new foal.
George is sampling home-brew from his vat.

June. Butterfly wings like ornamental shutters. Day scorches
down to diamonds, rubies before being lost at sea.
George is picnicking with friends on Rackwick beach.

July. Another wide-eyed sun. Its gold slick pours like oil
on the untroubled waves. Shoppers dab brows as they gossip.
George is drafting poems in a bottle-green shade.

August. Pudgy bees in romper suits suckled by flowers.
Well water rationed. Trout gills barely splashed.
George is hiding from the tourists' knock.

September. A brace of wrapped haddocks on the doorstep.
Mushrooms, snapped off under grass tufts, melt in the pan.
George is stocking up his shed with coal and peat.

October. Porridge and clapshot weather. Swan arrivals, divers.
Sun hangs, a smoking ham, suspended in the misty air.
George is ordering a hot dram at the pub.

November. Rain shaken out slantwise like salt. Hail pebbles
flung against the window to announce winter's return.
George is adding a wool layer to his clothes.

December. Three strangers, bearing gifts, enquire the way
to byre and bairn. A brightness absent from the map of stars.
George's craft is grounded among kirkyard rocks.

Delegates

Today, we have no responsibility for the world.
We are in transit between airport lounges.
It is Tuesday in one jurisdiction, Monday in another.
We cannot be tied down, we are on the run like fugitives,
sheltered by date lines and time zones, escaping tax
regulations, weather alerts, dodging the present tense.

*

Container boats – ferrying
imports, exports – can be
seen from our mezzanine.

A backdrop to negotiations
like a painted seascape
framed on an office wall,

turned to when minds wander
or memories are rifled
for near-precedents.

*

A strategic break. Mass migration towards the wash room.
A lemon squirt from your shrivelled member, then out again
to drum up support for your proposal: hands, perfumed
with liquid soap, gesture as you outline your rationale.

*

Always a harried official,
plastic ballpoint in mouth
like a thermometer, checking

the viability of a draft
beginning with the words,
'Notwithstanding the provisions of . . . '

                    *

An end-of-term mood
in the July conference rooms:
microphones switched off,
booth lights dimmed,
the open spaces
of the corridors
thinned of population,
attachés pressing 'o1'
in the mirrored lifts,
interpreters returning
to their mother tongues.

                    *

Friday night delays
of flights to capitals
by national carriers,
the wait for take-off clearance.

Jackets folded, stowed with duty-free,
balding heads lie back,
soak up news distributed
by smiling cabin crews.

                    *

Rushing the glass
            arrivals door,
you pick your
            expectant daughter

from the throng,
          playschool painting
elevated at the barrier
          like a name-board.

Buying a Letterbox

Another mouth to feed.
Our best face
turned to the world,
catching the brass
eye of the sun.

Should we buy the type
that snaps shut,
a trap scattering
bills and final reminders
like feathers, fur?

Or the limper kind
that yields easily,
tongue slobbering around
the postman's hand,
yet still eats anything,

digesting the bad news
as casually as the good?

Weather Permitting

I

The August day you wake to takes you by surprise.
Its bitterness. Black sullen clouds. Brackish downpour.
A drift-net of wetness enmeshes the rented cottage,
towels and children's swimwear sodden on the line.

Dry-gulleted drains gulp down neat rain.
Drops bounce from a leaking gutter with hard,
uncompromising slaps: and, like resignation
in the face of death, you contemplate winter

with something close to tenderness, the sprint
from fuel shed to back door, the leisurely
ascent of peat smoke, even the suburban haze
of boiler flues when thermostats are set.

You warm to those thoughts as you sit there,
brainstorming ways to keep the family amused,
plans abandoned for barefoot games on dry sand.
Handcraft shops? Slot-machine arcades? Hotel grills?

In truth – manipulating toast crumbs backwards,
forwards at the unsteady table's edge – you'd prefer
to return to your bed as if with some mild
ailment, pampered by duvet, whiskey, cloves.

II

Let it rain.
Let the clouds discharge their contents like reserve tanks.
Let the worms burrow their way to the topsoil
from whatever dank Sargasso they were spawned in.
Let dampness rot the coffin-boards of the summer house.
Let the shrubs lose their foothold in the wind,
the nettles lose their edge, the drenched rat
with slicked-back hair scuttle to its sewage pipe.
Let the tropical expanses of the rhubarb leaves
serve as an artificial pond, a reservoir.
Let the downpour's impact on the toolshed be akin
to the dull applause on an archive recording of a love duet.
Let the bricklayers at the building site wrap
pathetic sheets of polythene around doomed foundations.
Let the limb ripped from the tree's socket
hover fleetingly in the air, an olive branch.
Let a rainbow's fantail unfurl like a bird of paradise.
Let a covenant be sealed, its wording watertight.
Let the floods recede.
Let there be light.

III *After Giacomo Leopardi*

The storm runs out of wind; nature, which
abhors a silence, fills the vacancy with birdsong.
Deserting the airless, low-ceilinged coop,
the hen repeats herself ad infinitum. Replenished
like the rain-barrels, hearts grow sanguine.

Hammering resumes. Humming. Gossip. Croons.
Sun strides down lanes that grass has repossessed,
takes a shine to the brasses at the hotel where,
by the window she thrust open, the chambermaid
is marvelling at the cleansed freshness, calm.

Balm of mind and body. Will we ever feel
more reconciled to life than now, ever
know a moment more conducive to new hopes,
eager beginnings, auspicious starts?
How easily pleased we are. Rescind

the threat of torment for the briefest
second and we blot out dark nights of the soul
when lightning flashes fanned by wind
ignited fire and brimstone visions.
Sorrow is perennial; happiness, a rare

bloom, perfumes the air – so that we breathe
with the ease of a camphor-scented chest
from which congestion has just lifted.
Lack of woe equates with rapture then,
though not till death will pain take full leave

of our senses, grant us permanent relief.

Churchyard View: The New Estate

Taking it all with us,
we move in.

*

On their side, inviolable silence.
On ours, hammering, pounding,
sawing, clawing out foundations
with the frenzy of someone buried alive.

*

We like our dead well-seasoned.
Newly-ground soil disturbs.

*

She could wind him round her little finger
that is now solid bone.

*

My halogen light with sensor
alert for resurrections.

*

Every crow suspected as a raven,
every pigeon inspected for vulturehood.

*

They mark their death-days among themselves,
bake a mud cake, make candles of wax fingers.

*

Young since they were born.
Young since they were teenagers.
Young since they staged a coming-of-age
bash in the tennis club hall.
Young since they played non-stop
basketball for charity sponsorship.
This being young could only go on for so long.

*

Our houses, giant mausoleums,
dwarf their tombs to kennels.

*

Crab-apple windfalls
at the cemetery wall
no one collects for jelly.

*

The churchyard in shadow
like a north-facing garden.

*

Our freehold title
when the mortgage is redeemed.
Their graves to be maintained
perpetually by bequests.

*

Call my wrong number
in the small hours of the night.
Remind me how bad
things might – will – be.

*

A lip-puffed, ear-blocked, glow-nosed
head cold is what they feel nostalgia for.

*

How much it took to sustain their lives:
heaps of gravel, travel coupons, steel pads,
roll-on deodorants, bran flakes, tampons.

*

The dead seem more at ease in autumn
as the time to hibernate comes near.

*

Written before they were born,
these books foretold
anxiety and strife and war.
And yet they were born.

*

In our pine bed, we hear them stir
when floorboards creak, pipes cheep.

*

The prehensile clasp of the dead
grasping at prayer books
with straw–yellow claws.

*

Most die over a lifetime.
Others die all at once,
missing in action.

*

Not a sole dipped in churchyard snow.

*

The child's coffin
like a violin case.
A pitch which parents' ears
can hear through clay.

*

Buried talents lie.
Hoards unexcavated by posterity.

*

Scan the obit columns, uniform as war graves.
Check the maiden names, the regretting children.
Whole cities and towns wiped out.
A plague on all your houses.

*

A hearse in rush-hour traffic:
a ghost at the feast.

*

Two sisters
who wished each other dead
languish side by side.

*

Plots divided like vegetable allotments.

*

All behind them now.
The blushed fumblings of sex.
Interventional radiology.
Expense account lunches.
Games of bridge.

*

Death is the aftertaste of life.

*

Those who fester better than others.
Those who manage it more neatly.
Those fussy about the order
in which their organs decompose.
Those who discover an aptitude for death
they never had for life.

*

The blackness of
the cemetery blackbird,
its song an octave lower.

*

Above prison-high walls,
the trees – up to their knees
in slaughter – protest their innocence
to the outside world.

*

Who had a crush on the girl
six headstones away.
Who couldn't muster
the courage.
Who wouldn't make
the first move.

*

Paupers' anonymous plots.
Families in layers like bunk beds.

Crypts where coffins rest
on shelves, left luggage.

The rusted, railed-off holdings
of those whose souls

appropriate a private
heaven for themselves.

*

Add the total suffering of these bodies.
Deduct their combined pleasure.
What doth it profit a man?

*

As you were built on bone,
your house was built on sand.
Not a stone will stand upon stone.

A painted wall is a white lie.
You will crumble to the ground.
Your house will sicken, die.

*

I stare at the graves
like a sailor gazing out to sea.

*

A skull smashed,
      the crust of concrete
is sledgehammered open –
      dust to dust –
welcoming an addition
      to the family.

*

For whom growing pains, walking frames,
crash diets, price rises, self-esteem
were live issues once upon a time.

*

Days when death comes so close,
you say No to life.
Days when you could show death
how to live.

*

Should this end in spring
when death is overwhelmed
by winding sheets of green?
Or Halloween when
I overnight with friends?

from Family Album

July. My mother and I are in the kitchen.
Sun, outlined behind mist, swaggers into view.
Radio tuned to Athlone for the requests show,
she soaks the charred saucepan to which
a crust of porridge sticks, scrapes laval
streaks from a blue-rimmed egg-cup, squeezes
a plastic bottle for the last dregs of detergent.

I dry the dishes, leave her then, stuffing the gullet
of a circular washing machine with clothes,
adjusting the crank on the manual wringer.
Russian vine invades the outdoor toilet,
loose newspaper headlining scandals, crimes.
In my spongy sandals, I walk the cinder paths
between sweet and sharp competing fragrances.

Morning glories tighten their grip. Spurred nasturtiums.
Lettuce hearts harden. Beyond the hedge, bordered by silk
poppies – red slept-in party dresses – the dip and rise
of headscarfed women cycling on high nellies to the town.
Sound waves of conversation ripple through the heat.
Insects hum like chainsaws in a rain forest. Larks
about their business. A moist rubber-mouthed frog.

And snuff of dog roses. And wasps on house calls.
And a sudden outburst of church bells. And great
surges of silence. And my sister's skipping rhymes.
And berries roasting on their stalks, like fish grilled
on the bone. And a grasshopper's rhythms, a bamboo
thwacked by a bored child along park railings.
And permed dahlias. And days and days and days of this.

*

No work. No school.
    Sunday, January 20th 1963.
Wary cars are testing
    fresh clots of snow.
Crinkled seals of ice
    unbroken on the puddles,
rain-barrel frozen tight,
    what might our outlook hold
when the icicle sword
    guarding the bay window
corrodes and we gradually
    drift apart?

*

No exams this year.
The summer break is under way.
Days are brimful of potential.
My father takes me on his sales drive
to small towns near the county border.

Broad face cleared of thistle-spiky
bristle by a safety blade
– worked up to a lather
with shaving stick and brush –
he is glowing with good health,

glad of the company, the chat.
We overtake a bakery van, almost
able to catch the doughy draught of soft
white bread, cracked terracotta crusts
we'd love to pick holes in.

A milk churn on a donkey cart;
the farmer – legs dangled next
to an outsize orange wheel – salutes.
Hay-scented air streams through
our side-windows like thyme.

Crops reach out with a flourish
or are raked and baled and bound.
We laugh at the clapboard church
we pass but cross ourselves nonetheless.
Guess how many dogs we'll see

between here and Clogheen?
We each make a stab.
Dogs asleep in dung-scabbed farmyards.
Dogs lunging from boreens at our tyres.
Dogs hobbled to inhibit straying.

Down one steep, narrow-waisted road.
Up another.
Tracing the stout-walled perimeters
of a demesne; the disused railway line
an abandoned, meandering, flower-hemmed lane.

Council men with drippy cans of bitumen
stand in the shade between potholes.
He is so alive, my father, he can talk, drive,
become animated about a gymnastic stoat,
lacy patterns sun stencils through the trees.

He smiles at some remark of mine.
Tonight, he will repeat it to my mother
as she fills the ringing tea pot
with hot water; and, dinner eaten, will
record it proudly in his diary like a sale.

*

A lashing wet February night. Cold jabs of wind.
I park my bike. Stark unholy rainwater rushes
down the gutters of my exposed nose.

What a miracle it would take to step back
into my leaky shoes and enter the bleak,
unheatable cathedral (mosaics of angels,

wings gold-tipped like nibs; statuesque Marys
sheltering beneath the cross's beams) with faith
as firm as mine was then; ending a retreat,

we elevated rosary beads and scapulars for blessing,
roused to 'Hail Queen of Heaven' at the organist's
first hint; incense like a whiff of paradise.

Then trailing the May procession on its petal-strewn route
through the seminary grounds, apple trees in blossom,
high schoolboy voices breaking into hymns. Women in veils

and Child of Mary gowns. Sodality banners. Papal flags.

*

No, maybe I won't opt for a liquorice whip
or a powdery flying saucer after all; I swap
my 6d coin, sporting a silver greyhound,
for a cream pie (enough pennies yet to buy
ten real-looking cigarettes at lunch-hour).

The upper crust of chocolate is flecked
with little coloured dots that give my tongue
a sandpapery feel, exactly like our cat's,
the goo underneath like chewy ice-cream
wedged into the sugary inlet of a cone.

Though I'm tempted to start from the flat
wafery bottom, squared out like graph paper,
I work down conscientiously from the top,
gapped teeth meeting no resistance.
I drag the pleasure out all the way to school.

                    *

Saturday morning, our father ferries us to town.
A pound of this, a scoop of that, from fragrant sacks
of seeds, pellets, phosphates, feeds in Sutton's yard.
A pair of brass hinges at Molloy's hardware.
The library's squeaky-clean linoleum for Enid Blyton's
Secret Seven, a doctor-and-nurse story for our mother,
our father wavering between two gory wars.

Salmon-coloured stamps licked into savings books.
The sweet, addictive smell of pulped sugar beet
wafting our way on a raft of factory steam.
Bills to pay for clothes we'd tried on appro.
Then back to the car, pulling faces at passers-by,
while our father eyes a rival's cabbage plants,
doused and counted into hundreds at the market.

A busker plays a tarnished trumpet. Hawkers gesture.
Capped men off country buses check used suits for thickness.
Half-heads, teaty bellies, hard-salt flanks, smoked streaky
grace Molony's bacon window. My brothers and I caffle,
tire, then face out racing clouds until the world begins
to spin – like when our father swings us to dizziness,
sets us down on the kitchen's unstable ground.

Nocturne

Time for sleep. Time for a nightcap of grave music,
a dark nocturne, a late quartet, a parting song,
bequeathed by the great dead in perpetuity.

I catch a glance sometimes of my own dead at the window,
those whose traits I share: thin as moths, as matchsticks,
they stare into the haven of the warm room, eyes ablaze.

It is Sunday a lifetime ago. A woman in a now-demolished house
sings *Michael, Row the Boat Ashore* as she sets down the bucket
with its smooth folds of drinking water . . .

The steadfast harvest moon out there, entangled in the willow's
stringy hair, directs me home like T'ao Ch'ien: *A caged bird*
pines for its first forest, a salmon thirsts for its stream.

FROM

Exemplary Damages
(2002)

Out of Control

Worry on, mothers: you have
good reason to lose sleep,
to let imaginations run riot
as you lie in bed, not counting sheep
but seeing sons and daughters
like lambs led to slaughter
in the road kill of Friday nights.

Remain on standby, mothers –
you never know your luck –
for the knock that would break
the silence like the shock
of a metallic impact against brick.
Keep imagining a police beacon,
a blue moon shattering the darkness.

Lie warily, mothers, where,
eighteen years before, conception
took place in the black of night,
a secret plot; wait restlessly,
as if for a doctor's test,
to find out whether
you are still with child.

Blood Relations

I

Who descended from whom.
Who has whose eyes.
Whose nose.
Whose bone marrow matches whose.
Whose blood group.
Viscous as crude oil.
Sticky situations.
Four times thicker than water.
Brought to boiling point
at the least slip of the tongue.

II

Blood is what earns you
a sponsor's place
at the baptismal font
cradling your newest niece;

or, sporting a paper crown,
the right to dish out breast of turkey
at the Christmas get-together,
test the firmness of pink ham;

the privilege to share
in triumph or disgrace,
put up bail, act as guarantor,
face the midnight call.

III

Cells dunked in plasma,
fruit in syrup.
Clots, blockages, oxygen loss.

Such scope for bad blood.
The potency to pump 8,000 litres in a day.
100,000 beats worth.

More than your hardening
arteries may find
the capacity to forgive.

Saturday Night Fever

Playing tonight at the X-Ray-Ted Club,
The Chemotherapies, drugged to the gills,
the lead singer's pate modishly bald.

And who will your partner be?
Alzheimer, the absent-minded type,
with the retro gear, everything a perfect mismatch?

Huntington, grooving his hippy-hippy-shake routine?
Thrombosis, the silly clot, trying to pull a stroke?
Angina, who can be such a pain, and yet is all heart?

Raynaud, decked in ice-blue, coolest kid around?
Dear sweet Emphysema, so exercised she hardly
has a chance to catch her second wind?

Cancer, the rogue, ever-gregarious, spreading himself
around, groping his way niftily to a breast?
Parkinson who is already restless for the next number?

They sweat it out all night under the lightning strikes
of strobe lights flashing like an ambulance – such fun
that nobody, as they groan with pleasure, dreams of sleep.

Years After

And yet we managed fine.

We missed your baking for a time.
And yet were we not better off
without cream-hearted sponge cakes,
flaky, rhubarb-oozing pies?

Linoleum-tiled rooms could no longer
presume on your thoroughgoing scrub;
and yet we made up for our neglect,
laid hardwood timber floors.

Windows shimmered less often.
And yet we got around to
elbow-greasing them eventually.
Your daily sheet-and-blanket

rituals of bedmaking were more
than we could hope to emulate.
And yet the duvets we bought
brought us gradually to sleep.

Declan and Eithne (eleven
and nine respectively at the time)
had to survive without your packed
banana sandwiches, wooden spoon

deterrent, hugs, multivitamins.
And yet they both grew strong:
you have unmet grandchildren,
in-laws you never knew.

Yes, we managed fine, made
breakfasts and made love,
took on jobs and mortgages,
set ourselves up for life.

And yet. And yet. And yet.

from Exemplary Damages

Our one true God has died, vanished under
a rainbow's arch, banished like a devil
scalded by holy water; but our lives remain
eternally precious in the eyes of man.

We love one another so much the slightest
hurt cries out for compensation: sprain your
ankle in a pothole and City Hall will pay
exemplary damages for your pains.

We are equal under law as we once were
in His sight – just as He kept tabs
on the hairs of our heads, the sparrows
surfing the air, we are all accounted for,

enshrined in police department databases,
our good names maintained by the recording
angels of mailshot sales campaigns,
rewarded with chainstore loyalty points.

                    *

How will there ever be goods enough, white goods,
dry goods, grave goods, munitions, comestibles,
to do justice to all the peoples of the world?

Enough parma ham, however thinly curled,
to serve with cottage cheese and chives
in the cavernous canteens of high-rise buildings?

Enough rubs and creams, suppositories and smears,
mesh tops and halter necks, opaques and sheers?
How will there ever be enough flax steeped for smart

linen suits, enough sheep shorn for lambswool coats,
enough goats for cashmere stoles to wear on opening nights,
enough cotton yarn to spin into couture tops, flak jackets?

And can we go on satisfying orders for baseball caps, chicken nuggets,
body toning pads, camomile salve for chapped lips? And what quantity
of dolphin-friendly skipjack tuna meets a sushi bar's demands?

And how much serviced land remains for leisure-centre building,
how much hardwood forest has been cleared for grazing, how many
quarries can still serve as landfill sites for agribusiness waste?

And will there be sufficient creatures left to brighten up
our morning drives with road kill? Will the fox's brush-fire
be extinguished, the hedgehog's yard-brush swept aside?

What hope of raw ingredients for peroxide bleach, wheelie bins,
beach thongs, gluten-free bread, protective welding masks,
trucks transporting cars like reptiles ferrying their young?

*

Let's call it a day, abandon
the entire perverted experiment,
refuse to collude any longer with
the crude manipulations of sex,
the need for extra housing stock,
the record pressure on hospital beds.

Scrap the misbegotten concept
altogether, let the noxious rivers
wind their serpentine way towards
the caesium-fished, oil-slicked sea,
the stores of pesticides evaporate
through the widening ozone hole.

Burn the lot, the speculative rot propagated
about extra-terrestrial intelligence,
the self-help books to combat fear and stress,
the rules for ethical genetic engineering,
the blunt facts about cloning, the Bible tracts,
the glib self-deceptive upbeat texts.

Take it away, the latest theory on
bowel cancer and stem cell research.
Tear from limb to limb the handbook
on palliative care with its matter-of-fact
chapters on genitourinary disorders,
charts for accurate measurement of pain.

Let's not bestir ourselves to purge
the unholy mess, our daily urge to dispose
of rosy tampons, soiled baby Pampers,
home-delivery pizza styrofoam,
the hardening mustard crust of sewage,
thirst-quenching diet Pepsi cans.

It was all destined to end badly, near
the reactor core; or at the city dump
where fridges pour out their gaseous souls
and black plastic sacks spill synthetic
viscera for pillaging shanty dwellers
to scavenge, reap what we have sown.

Missing God

His grace is no longer called for
before meals: farmed fish multiply
without His intercession.
Bread production rises through
disease-resistant grains devised
scientifically to mitigate His faults.

Yet, though we rebelled against Him
like adolescents, uplifted to see
an oppressive father banished –
a bearded hermit – to the desert,
we confess to missing Him at times.

Miss Him during the civil wedding
when, at the blossomy altar
of the registrar's desk, we wait in vain
to be fed a line containing words
like 'everlasting' and 'divine'.

Miss Him when the TV scientist
explains the cosmos through equations,
leaving our planet to revolve on its axis
aimlessly, a wheel skidding in snow.

Miss Him when the radio catches a snatch
of plainchant from some echoey priory;
when the gospel choir raises its collective voice
to ask *Shall We Gather at the River?*
or the forces of the oratorio converge
on *I Know That My Redeemer Liveth*
and our contracted hearts lose a beat.

Miss Him when a choked voice at
the crematorium recites the poem
about fearing no more the heat of the sun.

Miss Him when we stand in judgement
on a lank Crucifixion in an art museum,
its stripe-like ribs testifying to rank.

Miss Him when the gamma-rays
recorded on the satellite graph
seem arranged into a celestial score,
the music of the spheres,
the *Ave Verum Corpus* of the observatory lab.

Miss Him when we stumble on the breast lump
for the first time and an involuntary prayer
escapes our lips; when a shadow crosses
our bodies on an x-ray screen; when we receive
a transfusion of foaming blood
sacrificed anonymously to save life.

Miss Him when we exclaim His name
spontaneously in awe or anger
as a woman in a birth ward
calls to her long-dead mother.

Miss Him when the linen-covered
dining table holds warm bread rolls,
shiny glasses of red wine.

Miss Him when a dove swoops
from the orange grove in a tourist village
just as the monastery bell begins to take its toll.

Miss Him when our journey leads us
under leaves of Gothic tracery, an arch
of overlapping branches that meet
like hands in Michelangelo's *Creation*.

Miss Him when, trudging past a church,
we catch a residual blast of incense,
a perfume on par with the fresh-baked loaf
which Milosz compared to happiness.

Miss Him when our newly-fitted kitchen
comes in Shaker-style and we order
a matching set of Mother Ann Lee chairs.

Miss Him when we listen to the prophecy
of astronomers that the visible galaxies
will recede as the universe expands.

Miss Him when the sunset makes
its presence felt in the stained glass
window of the fake antique lounge bar.

Miss Him the way an uncoupled glider
riding the evening thermals misses its tug.

Miss Him, as the lovers shrugging
shoulders outside the cheap hotel
ponder what their next move should be.

Even feel nostalgic, odd days,
for His Second Coming,
like standing in the brick
dome of a dovecote
after the birds have flown.

Heat Wave

Heat brought the day to its senses.
We are not used to such direct
expressions of feeling here
with our wishy-washy weather,
our dry intervals and showers,

our clearance spreading from the west;
rain and shine – ham actors –
mixing up their lines.
But there it was, the real thing,
an unstinting summer day,

not rationing its latitude for heat,
not squeezing out its precious metal
meanly between cracks in cloud.
Sunflower dishes tracked a solar path
across the radar screen of sky.

Apples swelled but still fell
short of breaking point.
The taut skin of black currants
would spurt open at a touch.
Ripening grain was hoarded

in the aprons of corn stalks.
A bee paused as if to dab its brow
before lapping up more gold reserves.
Tar splashed the ankles of cars
as they negotiated honey-sticky routes.

Foxglove, ox-eyed daisy, vetch
jostled for attention on the verges.
Spiders hung flies out to dry.

A coiled snake – puff adder
or reticulated python – would

have thrived in that environment,
mangoes supplanting gooseberries.
Were the river not reduced
to the faintest trickle of juice
it might have furnished

cover for a Nile crocodile
with sloped back patterned
like heat-soaked patio bricks.
A sudden low-lying cat dashed
between houses like a cheetah.

Had that sun made itself heard
it would have sounded like the inner
ferment of a cask of vintage wine,
the static on a trunk-call line
when someone phones out of the blue . . .

Birds retreated into silence, perched
deep inside leaf-camouflaged trees,
having nothing meaningful to add,
no dry-throated chalk-screeching
jungle note that would fit the bill.

A day that will spell summer always
for the child, too young to speak,
who romped outside among flower beds,
his mother's voice pressed thin and flat
as she summoned him languidly back

to the cool, flagstoned kitchen,
ice-cream blotches daubed
like sun block on his pudgy face.

Tulipomania

And who on earth would blame them,
those Dutch merchants prepared
to give up everything they owned
for the pearl of great price
that is a tulip bulb?

What house wallowing in canal mud,
like a rigged-out ship marooned
in harbour, could hold its own,
however secure its moorings,
against the ground-breaking tulip egg
that incubates in spring, sprouting shoots
of incandescent plumage: tangerine feathers
rippled with pink, streaked with aquamarine?

And who, with his priorities in place,
would hesitate to exchange
his very home for the tulip that leaves
no blood-red trail of perfume
but proceeds to make its bed
in the tactile gloss of satin sheets?

What crinoline gown, what silk
chemise, slithering to the boards
of a lead-windowed bedroom,
could compare with this stranger
bearing arcane knowledge from
a stream-splashed crag in Tien Shan
or the snow-melts of Tashkent?

Who wouldn't want to fade out
in a blaze of glory? Who wouldn't
sacrifice himself on an altar

of urn-shaped tulips, a pyre
of flaming crimsons, smoky maroons?

Who wouldn't be the better
for the lesson of those petals,
dropping off like share values,
precious metal rates,
leaving time to meditate on fortune,
speculate on loss?

Love Life

You really have to hand it to them.
They let nothing stand between them
and love's work; even in the face
of inequality and AIDS, admit
no impediment that would detract
from glossy theories of attraction
(*Put your seduction skills to the test
with this month's questionnaire . . .*),
'love' and 'forever' sharing the one
sentence like a king-size bed.

You really have to marvel at men
chivalrous enough to let themselves
be mesmerised by model bodies
conjured up on websites,
at women brushing up techniques
to keep their men on side,
despite courtroom reports

of barring orders, statistics
for divorce, incompatibility
on housework rotas, sport.

You have to recognise
the nobility in this busy,
cost-effective era of devoting
tranches of scarce time resources
to nail-painting, e-mail vigils,
rose bouquets, singles dinners,
basement bars, lace uplift bras,
discounting the mounting evidence
of chins, thinning crowns, downward
projections for the future.

You have to concede the idealism
it takes to get dressed up
to impress, then divest each other
of glad rags, down to the last
sad tufts of private hair; in an age
of hygiene hyper-awareness
to allow tongues explore where they will
as the muscular grip of the heart
tightens with excitement, a breaking
bag of waters ready to let rip.

Miraculous how the old ways survive:
gazing into another's eyes like precious
stones – spurning scientific findings
about hormones, seminal vesicles,
gametogenesis, selfish genes.
Voices dim, discreet as recessed
lights, over a bistro meal;
aired confidences, bared souls;
fingertips meet on the wine-stained
gingham cloth, feet entwine.

And so a new generation comes round
to the problem pages of teen magazines,
mastering the body-language needed
for hanging out at shopping mall
McDonald's or music megastore,
navels pierced, tiny skirts and shiny
cropped tops sneaked to weekend clubs,
unknown to parents offered curt
assurances about who'll be where
tonight, who with, till when . . .

And so your grandparents' names
are back in fashion, your twinkly
grandparents by whom the word 'sex'
was never expressed in your hearing,
whom you could never remotely imagine
making what we now call love.
'Still going on', as the great,
supposedly fouled-up Philip Larkin
(in an entirely different context)
wrote, 'all of it, still going on!'

The Clericals

How slowly, in those pre-flexi days, the cautious hands
of standard-issue civil service clocks moved, leaving you
impatient to change into flowered polyester frocks,
cheesecloth skirts, bellbottoms, platform shoes,
finding the sequinned night still young at 2 AM,
held in its velvet embrace under the gaze
of a ballroom's crystal moon, a disco's excitable lights.

Marys, Madges, Kathleens, it seems an age
since you guarded public hatches or sat in cream
and mildew-green gloss-painted offices, updating
records, typing carbon-copy letters on demand
for bosses, serving them leaf tea, checking the tot-ups
for payment warrants on slim adding-machine rolls,
date-stamping in-tray correspondence, numbering files.

The years have not been at all kind to you.
Your lives have not withstood the test of time.
not a spare cardigan draped on a chair-back,
not a card-index, not a hard-copy file remains
from the glory days of 1970-whatever when
your generation held the monopoly on being young:
twenty-firsts, all-night parties in a friend's friend's flat . . .

Your youth was snatched from your manicured grasp,
lasting no longer than the push-button hall lights in red-brick
houses where you returned by taxi in a pay-day's early hours,
barely allowed time to step inside and locate your bedsit key
before the darkness resumed: you unlocked the warped
plywood door in the eerie silence of a sleeping corridor,
set the fluorescent alarm clock on the prowl for morning,

undressed, flopped on the foam mattress, dreamt.

from Full Flight

All eyes on the annunciator screen, families
locate their check-in bay, before passing through
the x-ray vetting and the plexiglas walkway
to lounge around Departures, dressed in loud
anticipation of another climate, the blow-dry hot-air
blast that will greet them on arrival like a tour guide.

Boarding, in row-order, is called for raucously
at last; carry-on bags are manoeuvred into
narrow bins or stored discreetly under seats,
duty-free vodka bottles jangling like foreign coins.
Belts snap shut, cameras are flashed, blockbusters
deposited on laps, children plied with puzzle books.

The in-flight magazine is yanked from its
elasticated pocket; newspaper readers settle
on sports; business-class curtains close ranks;
a mix-up in a seat allotment is resolved.
Film themes and jazzed-up classics serve
as ambient music, the plane swerving into action.

Mist lifts from runway grass; a wedge
of leftover moon nestles on a shelf of cloud.
Engines gather the reckless speed
needed to raise wings to a higher plane,
to take off from the long flight path
of the tarmac, a dead-end country lane.

Below the dimmed cabin, a miniature
world – every detail faithfully reproduced –
can now be spied: rivers slop out into the tide;
lakes are potholes gouged in buckled mountains.
Then the land draws a borderline in sand.
Out on a limb, dangling over water,

nothing is seen except waves shuffling
their packs, the metallic dazzle of sea
like the video screens – as yet blank –
on which in-flight movies will be viewed.
The cabin crew, patrolling their beat, smile.
Passengers relax, take the weight off their feet.

*

From there, the world is recreated as collage:
waves like a cancelled air mail letter
the artist includes for its ethereal blues.

Then inland over glued-on fields:
wheat a yellowing newspaper page,
furrows the strings of a Picasso guitar.

*

Casting cloud aside
        like passive smoke,
the descending plane
        dips to an elevation
where the Atlantic's
        chop-and-change
is witnessed from
        the safe distance
of a window seat's
        reviewing stand,
a gold coast of sand
        outlined by yellow
highlighter pen:
        stepped waves,
boats towing
        trails of foam.
Then tufted fields
        crop up; wheels

put out feelers,
      anxious to
touch down
      on solid ground.

        *

Having retrieved their sliding cases from the carousel,
they leave the steel-clad baggage hall, declaring nothing,
follow trolleys to where tanned holiday rep,
regional HQ driver or exiled daughter waits;

then proceed beyond car rental stands,
tourist reservation booths, bureaux de change,
out into the shock of open air, the stink
of kerosene, the racket of taxis echoing

through the underpass, of courtesy coaches,
terminal shuttles . . . They have arrived.
Ears still popping, they make small talk,
unzip a purse or money-belt for local bills.

Now they are part of the ring-road traffic
they had pitied from the air, barely moving,
cogs in concrete wheels, passing vast hangars,
double-glazed houses devalued by flight-path noise.

Sheraton registers its name repeatedly in neon:
inside, uniformed crews are allocated rooms;
a bleary wayfarer, all the day's connections missed,
checks in for sleep. Travellers go on being routed,

defying laws of gravity, the risks of law-defying
hijackers, of pilot error, radar failure, lightning storms,
metal fatigue, having confirmed their ETA by air-phone
to grounded office colleague, lover, spouse.

In Town

The wizened country woman
with smoke-tanned skin
is foraging for provisions
among supermarket shelves.

Her floral headscarf is
as broad as it is long,
her fur-trimmed coat
a hand-me-down,

brown bootees patched,
the bag with her
pension money
darned at the strap.

When she pays
at the checkout
for oat flakes, stock
cubes, baking soda,

a cake jammed
inside pink icing,
she is ready for home,
all set for her cottage

along a back-road
that hedges its bets
between the clapped-out
sandpit and the handball alley.

A crocked Ford car,
abandoned by her son,
waits faithfully on
its pedestal of blocks.

Her sheepdog noses weeds
like an ant–eater
or snaps at a passing tractor
to speed it on its way.

Lean cows graze nearby:
udder bells – wind
chimes – brush against
rushes, wildflowers.

Thistles burst open
like worn sofas,
their downy stuffing
puffs and blows.

She keeps a holy water
font topped up, a gleaming
set of willow pattern,
a leatherette car seat

to put visitors at ease,
enough dry peat to see
her comfortably through
an average winter.

She is on her bike now,
the talon of the carrier
safeguarding her groceries
in an iron grip.

While Stocks Last

As long as a blackbird
still mounts the podium
of the aspen tree, making
an impassioned plea for song.

As long as blue tits, painted
like endangered tribesmen,
survive in their rain-forest
of soaking larch.

As long as the trilling lasts
above the office car park
and hands tingle to inscribe
in the margins of buff files,

'The skywriting of a bird
is more permanent than ink'
or 'The robin's eagle eye
questions these projections.'

England

Without nostalgia who could love England?
                                    – ANNE STEVENSON

Somewhere out there, England lingers
under the bushy brow of thatch that juts
above half-timbered houses in Home Counties.
A mill village survives where a raft
of flag irises rises near the grain loft
and the vicarage garden party is tastefully
announced on a hand-painted sign.
A family pile in Queen Anne style,
available at a knock-down price,
catches the needle-sharp eye
of a Lloyd's 'name' in the auction pages
of *The Field* or *Country Life*.
The hand-crafted. The home-made. The family-run.
Pink briar roses sink their claws
– like painted nails – into the gable walls
of listed cottages at Winchelsea and Rye.
Jersey cream dissolves in steaming scones
at the Salvation Army cake sale.
A smell of new-mown hay, of boiling jam,
of hops vented through an oast house cowl.

England is still out there somewhere,
an owl roosting in a cobwebbed barn.
You can overhear a pub argument about
the best brew of beer, best-ever shepherd's pie.
Alistair Cooke is delivering his four millionth
'Letter from America'; so many record-breaking
West End performances of 'The Mousetrap' or 'Cats';
the ten thousandth revival of 'An Inspector Calls'.
Tin-plate, ration-coupon laughter from the audience
of a radio panel show; Lilliburlero marching

on the BBC World Service, Big Ben chiming
to the second with the tea-time news,
the sig tune for 'Coronation Street' a national anthem.
Johnners greets listeners from Lords
as sunlight is rolled out along striped grass.
The tabloids have murder in their hearts.
That and exclusive photos of the latest
female tennis sensation at wet Wimbledon.
Scoreless draws in the Premier League.
Soft going at Newbury and Kempton Park.
Rain stopping play at a county cricket fixture.

Pastel-painted timber seaside chalets.
Miles of white clifftop caravans like dumped fridges.
A day-trip across ridged Channel waves:
cheap pints of bitter in the car ferry bar,
chips with everything in the cafeteria.
English Breakfast Served All Day in Calais.
Vera Lynn. VE celebrations. Our finest hour.
Poppy wreaths, brittle as old majors'
bones, wilt beneath the stony-faced
gaze of the Great War memorial.
Shakespeare settings by Roger Quilter
and Gerald Finzi in aid of the church tower
restoration fund, the vicar's wife doing
the page-turning needful for the accompanist.
A few tremble-lipped parishioners, feeling
their age, clear throats as the harmonium
is tuned and lend their bronchial best
to 'The Day Thou Gavest, Lord, is Ended'
while watery light through leaded glass
lands, like a housefly, on the brass plate
commemorating the valiant dead of Ladysmith.
Elgar's 'Pomp and Circumstance' arranged
for the Queen's visit by the colliery band.
Ralph Vaughan Williams's 'The Lark Ascending'

in rehearsal at the Free Trade Hall.
Gurney's Severn mists, Housman's blue
remembered hills, Hardy's wind and rain.
A Wilfred Owen troop train falling silent
at an unscheduled stop; or Edward Thomas's
halting express at Adlestrop taking on board
a consignment of pre-war blackbird song.
A brawny chestnut shields the clover-fattened
cattle in a hedgerowed field from searing noon.
Water-colour enthusiasts choose the ideal
viewing point to capture the flamboyant sunset.

The quiet courtesies. The moderation.
The pained smiles. Things left unsaid;
passed over in silence, an unwritten constitution.
Miles of graffitied tower blocks, near treeless
motorways wide as triumphal boulevards.
Race riots in Brixton and the North.
The peal of street-pleasing steel bands at Notting Hill.
Allotment cabbages with gaping caterpillar wounds.
Words like *tavern* and *shires* and *lea*.
Blazered Henley. Top-hatted Ascot.
Black herringbone for the Royal enclosure.
The wine-jacketed coach driver pointing
his blue-rinse passengers to the loos.
A single-room supplement for Christmas
at a refurbished Grand Hotel in some down-at-heel,
sea-eroded, once-genteel Edwardian town.

Romantic England is neither dead nor gone,
nor with Olivier in the grave.
It is out there somewhere still; plain-speaking
Stanley Baldwin's 'corncrake on a dewy morning,
the sound of the scythe against the whetstone . . .
a plough team coming over the brow of a hill'.
Homely John Major's England still holds its own

somewhere: 'long shadows on county grounds,
warm beer, invincible green suburbs, dog lovers'.
Goodly, portly Sir John Betjeman envisions his England:
'oil-lit churches, Women's Institutes, modest
village inns . . . mowing machines on Saturday afternoons'.

It is somewhere at the back of the mind,
like the back of a newsagent's where plug
tobacco is sold; shining like the polished
skin of a Ribston Pippin or Worcester Pearmain.
It preys on imagination, like pleated ladies
sporting on bowling lawns; like jowelled men
of substance nursing claret in oak-panelled
smoking rooms of jovial private clubs.
See it all for yourself – the quadrangled choir school,
the parterred garden with the honesty box,
the fox-hunting colonel on his high horse,
the Gothic Revival haunt leading through
a topiary arch to gazebo, yew maze,
pet cemetery – on your jaunts about
cobbled market towns, treks down lanes
rutted with what surely must be haywain wheels.

Listen to England as it thunders from Pennine becks
like a loud speech heckled by a Hyde Park crowd.
Listen to its screaming day traders, its bingo callers,
its Speaker demanding 'Order!' in the lower chamber.
Listen to the big band music to which couples
relax at the Conservative Club dinner dance.
Listen to the wax of silence harden
round the red leatherette upholstery
after closing time at the Crown and Rose;
steel shutters come down hard on the Punjab Balti;
grease congeals on the mobile kebab stall.
Listen to the tick of its Town Hall clocks,
like a Marks and Spencer shirt

drip–drying above a chipped enamel bath.
Listen to the silence in which England finds its voice.
It declaims this sceptered isle, this earth of majesty.
It claims some corner of a foreign field.
It chants while the chaffinch sings on the orchard bough.
It chants history is now and England.
It pleads green and pleasant land.
It pleads for all its many faults.

No, Thanks

No, I don't want to drop over for a meal
    on my way home from work.
No, I'd much prefer you didn't feel obliged
    to honour me by crashing overnight.
No, I haven't the slightest curiosity about seeing
    how your attic conversion finally turned out.
No, I'm not the least bit interested to hear
    the low-down on your Florida holiday.
No way am I going to blow a Friday night's freedom
    just to round out numbers at your dinner table.
No, I'm simply not able for the excitement
    of your school-term coffee mornings.
No, strange though it may seem, your dream kitchen
    holds no fascination whatsoever for me.
No, there's nothing I'd like less than to get
    together at your product launch reception.
No, I regret I can't squeeze your brunch into my schedule
    – you'll be notified should an opening occur.
No, I don't appear to have received an invitation
    to your barbecue – it must have gone astray.
No, my cellphone was out of range, my e-mail caught a virus,
    I had run out of notepads, parchment, discs, papyrus.
No, you can take No for an answer, without bothering
    your head to pop the question.
No, even Yes means No in my tongue, under my breath:
    No, absolutely not, not a snowball's chance, not a hope.

Not Yourself

Monday, you take the accordion out of its case in rain,
                              begin to busk.
Tuesday, you complain that the raïto sauce with your hake
                              is far too garlicky.
Wednesday, you temp as a PA in a software solutions firm,
                              filing your cherry-red nails.
Thursday, you will be the youth arranging for his sailboard
                              to be tattooed with a nude.
Friday, you gain consciousness after your last-chance operation
                              to beat prostate cancer.

Monday, you will be a gate-leaning farmer, watching tall wheat
                              ripen like bamboo.
Tuesday, you are on duty at the beauty salon, adding volumising
                              shampoo to crestfallen hair.
Wednesday, you will be fitted with a spinal stimulator, if metabolic
                              complications are resolved.
Thursday, you are a salesman picking your teeth as you leave
                              a small-town hotel.
Friday, with your fellow-envoy, you try your damnedest to revive
                              stalled peace negotiations.

Monday, you joke with other widows about the bloke who calls
                              the bingo numbers.
Tuesday, you are a parcel-lumbered motorcycle courier,
                              jousting with gridlock.
Wednesday, you will block the undertaker's lane, unloading
                              a consignment of veneer.
Thursday, you stack up cushions for a clearer view from the seat
                              of your adapted car.
Friday, you will attack defence computer systems worldwide
                              with your virus.

Monday, you bring the best case you can to the attention of
                           the sentencing review board.
Tuesday, you lock yourself inside an orthopaedic corset to save
                           your back from strain.
Wednesday, your slow fast-lane driving is greeted with the accolade
                           of a two-finger salute.
Thursday, you know the acute pain of seeing your new purchase
                           at half the price you paid.
Friday, you administer morphine to a doubly incontinent patient
                           in a dank public ward.

Monday, you will iron white shirts like a carpenter
                           planing a plank of deal.
Tuesday, you feel a cold coming on as you banter to your passengers
                           on the tour coach.
Wednesday, you will broach the subject of a barring order
                           with your younger kids.
Thursday, you will change into uniform before collaring
                           your guard dog for patrol.
Friday, you will wake up stark naked, wearing only
                           your lover's arm.

Monday, you are a leotard-clad ballet dancer rehearsing
                           for *Coppelia* at the barre.
Tuesday, you are a car mechanic in a pit: dirt infiltrating skin,
                           grit irritating a graze.
Wednesday, you are the mindless old man whose happy release
                           his family prays for.
Thursday, you will give birth to a child, smuggled like a refugee
                           under your tarpaulin.
Friday, you will struggle across the fairway, humping your golf bag
                           like an oxygen tank.

Monday, either as a bank's investment analyst or flipping burgers
                           in a fast-food chain.
Tuesday, the unsame . . .

At the Seminar

I

An electronic blip from house-martins as they pass
an open window at the conference centre; frantic birds,
on errands of mercy, transporting relief supplies to tricorn beaks.
We sneak a glance at our mobiles for text messages.

Crawling across the hotel lawn, sun puts mist in the shade:
a transparent morning now, our vision unhindered for miles.
A golfing party, armed with a quiver of clubs, aims
for the bull's-eye of the first hole; others, near a pool
blue as our EU flag with its water sparkle of stars, dry off:
shrink-wrapped in towels, they sink back into resort chairs.

II

For serious objective reasons, we are informed, our keynote
speaker is delayed; the Chairman's interpreted words
are relayed simultaneously through headphones:
In order to proceed to a profitable guidance for our work
which will be carried out with a feature of continuity and priority ...

I see the lake basking in its own reflected glory, self-absorbed,
imagine turquoise dragonflies, wings wide as wedding hats,
fish with scarlet fins, water-walking insects.

I intervene. I associate myself with the previous speaker's views.
Discussions go on in all our languages as I unscrew
still mineral water, bottled at some local beauty spot.
Certain administrations suffered cuts as they weren't entrusted
with new attributions likely to fill in the logistical gap
resulting from the inference of the frontierless economic area ...

In two hours (less, if – with luck – that stupid clock has stopped)
our final workshops will convene in the break-out rooms.
Then it will be time to draw conclusions at the plenary,
score evaluation forms, return to our respective floors
to dress down for the bus tour of the Old Town.

III

Now the rapporteurs start synopsising
the workshop findings on felt-tip flip-charts.
The Chairman is summing up: *New challenges*
overlook the world scenery in our global stance . . .

Lily pads strut across the lake like stepping stones;
fish risk an upward plunge; martins – plucking
sustenance from thick air – lunge at their mud nests.
Hold the world right there. Don't move a single thing.

Germ Warfare

As saints kissed lepers' sores, caressed rank beggars' wounds,
    I ought to thank God for the way you
    Spray me with your germs, my fellow travellers.
I should take it like a seraph, or at least like a man,

Ingest your pestilence with relish, meditate indulgently
    On sprinklers dousing a striped lawn,
    Feel proud to hothouse your viruses in my lungs,
Pick up stray bugs like hitchhikers, pets needing a good home.

So by all means go on sneezing in that spunky style of yours:
    The convulsion, the eruption, the paroxysm, the pile-drive,
    The dog yelp, the orgasm, the gale force, the squelch,
The caught short, the sudden brake, the snort, the screech owl.

Let it all hang out, therefore, whatever it happens to be.
    You with the unprotected schnozz, as though a hanky's
    Prophylactic would sin against your principles, your faith,
You who pass your plague around like cough drops,

You can be relied upon to prop yourself beside me
    On the bus, telling your cellphone how much
    You suffer, as you present me with hard evidence,
Certain that a problem shared is a problem halved.

The morning before the long plane journey, the crucial interview,
    The special date, whenever hoarseness begins to tighten
    Round my throat like a noose, thoughts wander back to you,
Eyes water, touched by the largesse with which you showered me,

Smitten to the core by your infectious charms. Bless you!

So Much Depends

The red barn. The Vermont farm
you fled from to the city
or vowed you'd retire to some day.

The barn at your grandparents'
in Kansas where you stowed away
one preteen summer, happy

to be left alone, at sea on the prairie,
hay spilling before cutter blades,
waves breaking on an inland shore.

A battened-down barn, holly-berry red
against the first dusting of snow.
Chevron-patterned wagon doors.

The grocery store forty miles off,
an upstate Amish village planted
among neat-drilled horse-tilled fields.

There will always be room
in the scheme of things for a red barn.
You may depend your life on it.

Inhale cured fodder, grain, manure.
Admit winter cattle to the stalls.
This is your clapboard cathedral:

pillars, nave, aisles, weather vane.
Wheat is separated from
chaff here, sheep from goats.

Come back, Grandma Moses, lead us
from the desert of downtown
to the promised land of the red barn.

Time Pieces

How long a day lasts.
It starts at dawn,
goes on all night,
right into the small
hours, makes time
for each minute
individually.

       *

How long days take.
An evening when you wait
for the phone to ring
as if for a watched kettle
to come gasping
to the boil and sing.
A week in which your lover
broods the situation over.
A summer marking time
before exam results.
The breathing space
the lab requires
to prove your GP
right or wrong.

*

The grandfather clock keeps
time under lock and key,
counts the seconds like a miser
inside walnut-panelled vaults.

Its chimes disturb light sleepers,
hold them in suspense
until another hour's demise
is hammered home.

*

The word *forever* as used
in a pop song chorus.
The word *vintage* as it occurs
in the second-hand shop-talk
of the clothes store – say, in
this label: *Vintage Slip, 1980s.*

*

When we settled in
        to the new house,
distancing ourselves
        from our sour past,
secure at last in exultation,
        we knew we would
never again be as young
        as we were then;
nor had we been for years.

*

My contributor's copy
of *The New Younger Irish Poets*
        already liver-spotted with age.

*

And to think
of her once-new
bijou town house –
sleek, chic, state-of-the-art,
latest in everything –
advertised for sale
'in need of modernisation'.

*

Seems only yesterday
you woke in this same
bedroom and dressed
for the same steady job,
here where you will wake
again for work tomorrow,
your yesterdays adding up
to thirty years of waking
since you were waved off
by hands it now takes
memory to flesh out.

*

Like the snow in Joyce's story
that falls all over Ireland,
on the living and the dead,
grey hair has lodged

on most heads of my generation
and the first flurries start
to take root in the next.

*

December 31st: punch line to your diary.
The date when time runs out.
When you may take your case no farther.
When you must sign off, watching your
dead – in passé glasses, retro gabardines –
lag farther behind, as you place your faith blindly
in a new year's resolution of your plot.

*

It comes almost as a relief,
the long-anticipated voice
creeping down the line:
the phone call you had
coming for a long time,
for years of nights;
a dark secret, a rodent
gnawing at your sleep.

*

Travel as a backward step.
You journey until you find
a meadow where wildflowers
grow with pre-factory-farming
copiousness, a horse-drawn
landscape where hay is saved
in older ways, to revive
the life you lived once,
catch up with your past.

*

Whatever it was you feared
has not come to pass.
Not tonight at least.
Whatever it is afflicts you
will not last.

Your siege will lift.
You will take the risk
eventually to say,
'Things really were unbearable
way back then.'

*

How briefly a day
lasts, unravelling so fast
you can't keep pace.
You are at the morning
bus stop, wondering
if you definitely
locked the hall door
when, what seems
like seconds later,
sunset struts by
in all its sky-draped
finery, its evening
wear, and you are
unlocking the hall door.

*

Wiping clean the day's dark slate,
sleep sweeps you off your feet,
leaves you dead to the world
in your bedclothes, shrouded in sheets.

Foreseeable Futures

(2004)

Life

Life gives
     us something
to live for:
     we will do
whatever it takes
     to make it last.
Kill in just wars
     for its survival.
Wolf fast-food
     during half-time breaks.
Wash down
     chemical cocktails,
as prescribed.
     Soak up
hospital radiation.
     Prey on kidneys
at roadside pile-ups.
     Take heart
from anything
     that might
conceivably grant it
     a new lease.
We would give
     a right hand
to prolong it.
     Cannot imagine
living without it.

Sermons in Stones

Mountain peaks
  aspire to wisdom.
Passing like molten
  glass through fire
and water, they thirst
  for knowledge
pure as driven snow.
   What mountains
know is gleaned
  from rifts and faults
and shifting plates,
  a faith moving
across millennia,
  sermons in stones
handed down
  in granite seams.
It is towards mountains
  that we lean
for answers,
  scanning their
weathered folds
  as if each
shimmering outcrop
  hinted at some
bedrock insight,
  gold reserves of truth,
looking to their
  carbon–dated strata
for the longer view.

Soft Fruit

The ephemeral life-cycle of a ripe raspberry,
its beady fruit an enlarged mayfly's eye,
everything about it tentative, dissolving
like an ice-cube in your palm, where you
toss one around absent-mindedly, content
to fritter away a sun-sated July day.

Filmy pink, styrofoam light, faintly obscene,
those atoms of fruit split between fingers,
smudge whatever surface they rub against.
Taste one and it makes a stab at bitterness
but proves too gentle for the role, a softie –
lush, slushy, surrendering to the condition of a jam:

a pulp, like treaded grapes, the seedy paste
bubbling in the hectic kitchen when steamy
windows must be sealed to keep out greedy,
sweet-toothed wasps ... Spice up your life
with madras, chased by a raspberry sorbet
or whip up a taste for raspberry crème brûlée.

Surrender. Feel hard-and-fast intentions melting
in the presence of a raspberry chocolate crunch sundae.
Drink to your own health with a brandy-based
raspberry liqueur that has come to fruition, matured
in heat, distilled near jam-jar traps on windowsills.
Hold back unblemished specimens for freezing,

for defrosting when icy winter bites: preserving
summer's patois, looking not the least
like clean-shaven apricot or pouting peach,
but (how appearances deceive!) as if each
were as burred as a cat's raspberry tongue –
the purring cat that scoffed the cream.

Brothers at Sea

We inlanders don't have a sea leg
to stand on when we laze along the prom,
unable to establish much rapport
with the hazy waves, unable to identify
the spiky birds that bob ashore,
then flap nervously elsewhere;
unwilling, in the stiffish breeze
ruffling the strand, to chance our arms
lying back on damp sheets of sand
in a wager that the sun might overwhelm
the heavy odds of cloud; nor will we throw
discretion to the winds – shed an anorak
or doff a cap – merely for the sake
of a cool holiday appearance.

Without surfboard, rod or dinghy
as prop, we lack an adult alibi
to match childhood's spade and bucket.
Should we roll up our trousers,
wade ankle-deep, risk letting water
steep our boneheaded knees?
We enjoy at best a nodding
acquaintance with the sea,
strictly restricted to summer,
limited to day trips, involving
hefty excavations of fresh air,
all-you-can-breathe ozone
densely textured as candy floss
sold in a slot machine arcade.

While there is the clear option
of training the coin-op telescope
on cliffs, our preference is for

rushing a limp vinegar–dripping
bag of chips and battered fish
to the snug car for a steamy meal,
then – irrespective of the weather –
to fall into line with a whipped
ice-cream cone for atmosphere,
letting the fussing, fretting waves
in the foreground create a scene.
We might down a beer in the Mermaid Bar,
pit ourselves against the rifle range
until the small change of our luck runs out.

Though we're ready to make our excuses –
that raw breeze, the forecast rain –
and all set for reversal from the sandy
car park, for easing our journey
home by the picturesque route,
we steal one more quizzical look
at the way those fleet-footed waves
tiptoe across the shore before, losing
balance, they fall flat and withdraw.
Shrieks of five-a-side beachballers
reach our wind-pummelled ears.
A shivering family gets into the swim.
Grasping for some final payback,
we stare as if anticipating revelation.

As if waiting for some explanation to sink in.

Natural Causes

Summer smells to high heaven
      like this lavender garden
where chilled nectarine soup
      infused with mixed-fruit
syrup and fresh mint
      spiked with more than
a hint of anisette liqueur
      is served on the lawn
while every blade
      of grass is ratified
individually by the sun.

                    *

Cézanne can bring himself to paint
only a corner of the summer farmyard.

This is as much as he can take in at once
such is the intensity of what he finds.

Wheat, ripening into Van Gogh yellow,
is lifted above the daily grind.

Monet, abroad at all hours with his easel,
traces the relationship of light and hay.

Stacks are shaped like sun-baked pies
packed for a crusty farm worker's lunch.

*

The conveyor
belt of spring
and summer
moves so fast
it soon reduces
flowers to rubble
in its impatience
to press onwards
along its petal-
strewn route,
its primrose path.
A smattering of
snowdrops melts.
Daffodils, yellow
chicks, lie bruised
and limp-necked.
Lilac, laburnum,
whitethorn flick past
like fabric samples.
Mangled cherry
blossoms fall as
polka dots on cars.
Nature – no soft touch
for sure – changes
its mind about
which pastel colours
it should favour
and moves
capriciously on:
fresh-faced flowers
barely stalked
within its sights
when they are mown
down in their prime.

*

Then the warm spell runs out of steam.
We must settle for mean temperatures,
a nip of autumn at the tips of branches,

the whole show folding its tent before our eyes,
leaving us cold, putting a damper on our hopes.
Some chill sense lingers that we have crossed

a boundary, are entering a final phase:
the frosty reception of breath at morning
like the plumes on a funeral carriage,

depressions circling the weather map,
storms at sea, ice inching along roads,
the slippery slope towards winter.

September

Late honeysuckle lushness.
Fields of barley bristle.
Oatmeal thrushes ransack berries.

Along a lane, cooking-apple green,
a mare – tail a sun-bleached
stook of corn – is reined in.

Mist has lifted from the river
which rides side-saddle across the weir.
The year has switched its engine off

to save fuel on the downward run,
revelling in every cloud-break,
in hailstones of grain,

lofty trailers of baled straw,
pyramids of peat storing
mummified winter heat.

Combine harvesters will soon
return to yards, like planes landing
at base after reconnaissance.

Bees devour nectar at a pace
scarcely concealing desperation.
Dipped in a stream, where willows bow,

deferring to their own reflections,
cows are herded from an Aelbert Cuyp
(one of those Dutch paintings that incite

art critics to cream off their richest
prose: *drowsy heat, dewy peace,*
golden calves, pleated water).

Gather blackberries while you may:
let loose their inky juices on blank vellum.
Illuminate your findings like a scribe.

Foreseeable Futures

I   *The New*

The distinctive
      Irish bungalow,
built by instinct,
      needing no plans,
just the heft
      of direct labour
and the odd day's
      back-up from
a local handyman.
      Look how quickly
it takes shape,
      breeze block showing
through plaster
      like visible panty line.

II   *Mid-Terrace*

With prices spiralling through the roof,
you could I suppose come round
to loving this lacklustre house
and such grounds as it stands on.
It's the best you can afford.

Maybe – if you decided to buy –
the wrought-iron staircase curlicues
would grow on you, the plywood veneer,
the tiled fireplace, the cemented-over garden
where you could almost squeeze the car.

III *Planning Permission*

Right at the corner of the lane
where the wren is feathering its nest
and the scent of hawthorn is a condiment
adding spice to spring, a planning notice

has been planted, staked down like a sapling.
You make the wary approach
of someone scrutinising a suspect
package, a booby-trapped device.

IV *Viewing Recommended*

Strutting about your house,
as though we already own it,
we find the place on best behaviour,
everything done and dusted.

We superimpose our lives
on your lives, paste our heads
on to your bodies, grind coffee
in your kitchen, hack back

your garden privet, make love
furtively in your bedroom
where the *en suite* tiles
leave much to be desired.

V *Testing*

The soil mechanics jeep makes a beeline
for the centre of the former wheat field.
Hard-hatted men are setting up equipment.
Wheat will have yielded to concrete
before the growing year is out.

Lord Mayo

You have come to a bad end, Lord Mayo,
to find yourself lodged in digs next to mine.
Yours is the grave my house looks down on.
Or would if your tomb could protrude
like a well-fed belly through your waist-band
of nettles and ground elder and brambles.

Fancy not having a lackey who can make
the railings stand to respectful attention,
keep you sealed off from mere mortals,
lend the rusted bars a bit of class with a dab
or two of paint, lop off that ridiculous
top hat of ragwort and silk poppies.

It's a strange reversal of the old order
that you should be mucked about
without frieze coat or gaiters, while we –
fast-forwarded a century and a bit later –
are double-glazed, centrally heated,
en suite'd, dry-lined, living it up.

What a state you are lying in,
for a man of your stature, having
shrunk to this rectangle smaller
than a billiard-room, your name the mud
of a poor Irish county, a bogged-down
empire on which the sun never rises.

Or – to be impertinent and frivolous at once –
it connotes the mayonnaise option at the sandwich
counter. And such chop-licking wraps,
such goat's cheese and aubergine melts,
such sushi specials and antipasto misto
are now served in our lunchtime delis.

You'll observe how uppity the peasants
have become: hurtling off-road 4 by 4s
(the new coach and four) from crèche
or ironing service, ordering carry-out
meals – Indian, Thai, Chinese – no less exotic
than florid shrubs uprooted from the colonies.

One thing, I'll say, Lord Mayo, in your favour:
song thrushes love to bits the berries
that sprout from your personal yew tree
(a yew that responds eerily to gales),
unbuttoning them lustily like a scullery maid
undone in some stately basement kitchen.

As for the elderberry bushes, clustered
at your feet like a pleated curtain
on a four-poster bed, how appropriate
in your lordly context is Heaney's image
elevating those ball-bearing berries to 'swart caviar'.
Use your silver coffin-plate for daintiness

when you scoop them up to taste: a dish fit for a king.

Seven Ages

Teens are wrapped round one another
like cars locked in the embrace of lampposts
after closing time in clubs and bars.

Twenties, having shacked up in a bedsit,
save for a house deposit and the outlay
for the full works on the Big Day.

Thirties – circumnavigating the neighbourhood –
are on the two-car shuttle between school gates,
face painting, violin lessons, junior sports displays.

Forties hope to prove themselves enlightened
when moping-and-tantrums syndrome strikes
their back-chatting, drumkit-bashing young.

Fifties, at leisure to relieve the child-minding
side of their children's pressures, wheel
squealing granddaughters to sleep in buggies.

Sixties try to ignore signs of decline but still
accept a sorely-needed lift from son or daughter
to the support-group meeting or out-patients' prefab.

Seventies blab on about deteriorating standards,
wish their children hadn't relocated at such distance,
live for Christmas reunions, bide their time.

Boy Singing Schubert

A late-night silence beds down
at that dreamy hour when house lights
dim to long-life bulbs on landings
and one day leads to another.

The silence of deepest cyberspace
to which unsaved data is consigned.
The flat summer silence of a midlands village –
canal barges tethered like donkeys,

tourists snug in pubs, swans at large
like spume trapped at a lock-gate.
The silence of a log-warmed farmhouse
overcome by fumes of snow.

                    *

The silence to which our class of raucous boys
was reduced when, pending our teacher's return,
one of our number started unexpectedly to sing.

Forehead pressed as firmly to the desk as an injured temple
to cool metal, he avoided eye-contact with our ridicule,
our scorn, concentrating solely on song:

peak notes ascending the halo-capped summit
of Mary's statue, flowers arranged as a May altar
at her clay feet – ruck-leafed primroses; bluebells

the sky-blue of tricky jigsaw pieces; dewy sprigs
of lilac plucked that morning. *Ave Mar-e-e-a, gratia plena,*
Dominus tecum, benedicta tu in mulieribus.

Free Range

A fistful of gold
       – chickenfeed –
doled out from a sack
       is enough to mobilise
a brazen procession of hens,
       falling into line,
feeding against the grain,
       then breaking ranks again,
drifting absentmindedly away.
       One goes chugging
towards the orchard
       where apple trees stoop
under the weight of fruit
       roosting in branches.
Another – taking wide, determined
       police-like strides –
hits upon an indefinite
       line of enquiry
as it vaguely scrapes
       evidence together,
scratches around for clues,
       peruses every last speck,
keeps its pecker up
       leaving no stone unturned.
And this one bobs
       above the wavery aftergrass,
bottle-top crown
       and foam-rubber wattle
an extravagant opera costume:
       a full-dress rehearsal as
it sounds that languid note
       always so evocative of summer

and leaves it floating
          in the air, dangling
by the skin
          of its hen's teeth.

Book Sale

          Seizing, as if in panic,
armfuls of reduced-price classics,
          bound in sombre, artful jackets,
he is determined at last to take
          a stand on *Crime and Punishment*,
come to terms with *The Rights of Man*,
          surrender to the power of *Leviathan*,
renew youth like a library book:
          remembered times past when –
cushioned from hardship, lying astride
          an easy-chair or in the wood-panelled
reading room of a summer garden lair,
          an aromatic tea chest marked *Ceylon*,
he plunged headlong into adventure,
          knowing contentment like the back
of his page-turning hand, oblivious
          to the rota of household chores,
the squeegee singing of a thrush,
          the tennis ball's monotonous crush
on a gable wall, the canter
          of an empty meat tin blowing
like perpetual motion near the bin,
          cows ripping out chapters of grass.

He expects more substance from
　　　　　his reading now, of course,
and these books he stacks up
　　　　　at the cash desk have a weighty feel:
You must change your life is what
　　　　　he wants to hear them say,
There is still time to begin.
　　　　　They will fill his shelves like resolutions,
tasks he must get round to some day soon:
　　　　　that leaking tap, that creaking door,
that bathroom fungus needing close attention.

Non-Stop Christmas

Christmas is always coming.
It steals sneakily up on you,
snapping at your heels, ready
to pounce like a pantomime wolf.
Or it looms ahead like a road block,
a juggernaut impossible to pass.

Christmas is always near at hand.
You find it lurking in the attic: hidden
with the Santa things you landed
at the right price in a summer sale;
lingering in the brittle fringes of the artificial
tree you store beside the water tank.

Christmas is always on the cards,
for the child addressing the North Pole,
for the emigrant booking tickets
on the no-frills airline website,
for siblings singing from different carol sheets,
raking over old coals at the hearth.

Christmas is always brandished above your head,
a carving knife; or it looks you sharply in the eye
like a tack with a rip of crepe paper attached
that brings garish paper-chains to mind in hazy July.
It tumbles from a cupboard in the shape of hoarded
decorations: folded golden tinsel concertinas.

It is always Christmas in the house
where a useless crewel-work gift can't
be disposed of tactfully, where broken
toys are tripped over, where the non-shed tree
needs to be stripped of glittering baubles
like a court-marshalled soldier's gongs.

Christmas is always showing its ugly face
like the switched-off neon Santa in the pub
left to drive his reindeers up the walls in summer.
A few unmelted flakes of fake snow hang on
for months to a corner of the butcher's window.
Extra tonic stocked in case of visitors goes flat.

The Christmas season is always declared open.
The word slips out with indecent haste in a TV
advertisement and when the hotel's securing deposit
for the office party must be rounded up by August.
Christmas is always striking like a seasonal virus.
There are only ever so many days still left.

Eel

after Eugenio Montale

Eel, wee sleeket
siren of icy seas,
lashing out
against the choppy
tide, slipping
from the iron fist
of Baltic waters,
unable to resist
the lure of distant
estuaries, streams
drenched in
freshwater perfumes,
not hindered
even by drought
when the trail
of current runs out
to a gravelly trickle,
muddy dregs of slime,
and the sunshine,
flooding a net
of chestnut trees,
throws light on
her inward advance:
eel, laser beam,
headstrong as a torch,
lean as a whip,
sharp as a love-
tipped arrow,
brooking no delay,
drilling to the core,
the pith, of rock,
flailing past

stagnant gullies,
sparking hopes
that counteract
the ashen heart
of darkness,
flashing like a
curled-up rainbow,
like the pools
of your green eyes,
and she mirrors
your every move,
proving you to be
– admit it –
her kinswoman,
her truest sister
under the skin.

Low-Fat

I worry like mad about
      the pork sausages man
I see some mornings
      unloading his refrigerated truck
when I am stuck in a backlog
      of commuter traffic.
He just doesn't seem at all
      cut out for the job,
not strong enough to be
      lugging those backbreaking
cartons – low-fat though
      some are labelled –
of gold-medal sausages,
      laden boxes
of hickory-flavoured rashers,
      too bashful to ignore
the way the shop owner –
      meeting demands for
newspapers and milk –
      hasn't a civil word to spare,
not brash enough to fob off
      the prowling warden
by lobbing an evil eye.
      He'll never hack it,
though he gives it his best,
      mimicking the gait
of a bigger man,
      owlish schoolboy glasses
flashing like gold medals
      above the tottering boxes
as a taxi horn taunts him
      for blocking rights of passage,

a bus driver gestures
        with two uplifting fingers,
a mounted policeman pounces
        from his motorcycle
and the fat is definitely
        in the fire this time.

The Light of Other Days

I freely admit to having always
detested John McCormack's voice:
the quivering tenor pitch,
the goody-good way he articulates
every in-dee-vid-you-al syllable,
prissily enunciating words
like an elocution-class nun.
And – though clearly not his fault –
the hiss on old 78s is oppressive
as if he had a fog (*sic*) lodged in his throat,
as if a coal fire in the parlour where
those songs supposedly belong
were leaking methane
through the gramophone horn.

Or perhaps that surface hiss
is the dust coating mahogany cabinets,
their Sunday-best hush
of wedding-gift china,
tarnished silver trophies,
inscribed retirement salvers,
cut-glass decanters
that have lost their shine;
the locked parlour gone musty
as the cover of Moore's *Melodies*
(shamrocks, harps and wolfhounds
wriggling their way out
from an undergrowth of Celtic squiggles).

McCormack's mawkish rendering
of *I Hear You Calling Me* nauseates
so much the gramophone could be
winding me up, deliberately needling me,

applying surface scratches to my body,
tattooing my skin with indelible images
from the Eucharistic Congress of 1932
when, for the mass congregation,
he sang *Panis Angelicus* in that
ingratiating way of his, sucking up to God.

Why do I bother my head tolerating
this travesty? Why don't I force him
to pipe down, snap out of my misery
like an 'Off' switch, send the record
spinning against the wall at 78 revolutions
per minute, rolling it like his
rebarbative 'r's before I throw?

Am I compelled to let it run its course,
an infection, wait until the stylus
lifts its leg to finish, because, well,
this sickly song calls back to mind
a father whose tolerance for such
maudlin warbling knew no bounds?
Could he, by some remote chance,
be the special guest expected indefinitely
in the stale, unaired parlour
laid with deep-pile carpets of grime?
Does McCormack's loathsome
voice succeed in restoring
that father figure, at least momentarily,
remastering him from dust?

The Home Town

Our town needed no attention from the fast-talking city, to boost
its self-esteem, shrugged off its lack of name-recognition status,
the absence of an entry in the standard tourist guidebooks.

Flash-flooded paddocks were the nearest we came to creating a
    splash.
The cathedral took tame inspiration from its Pisan counterpart.
Our hill quarried for silky lime would scarcely warrant a coach tour.

To while away spare time, there were Sales of Work in aid of
    foreign
missionaries, mixed doubles golf competitions, Lenten plays, clay
    pigeon
shooting tournaments, the New and Capitol cinemas to view films.

Had your parents not exercised the hard choice on your behalf,
you might not – all things considered – have settled on it as the first
spot on earth you'd opt for as a birthplace; but it more than sufficed.

And a bond deepened between you: you responded to its easygoing
    wit,
its readiness to lift a hand, took pride in its sizeable stadium, watched
the river flee beneath the bridge like a non-stop mainline train.

          *

Hardly a day passes that the town does not cross your mind,
and though, officially, you've left behind the confines of its square,
acquired what lawyers call new domicile, it still answers to home.

And when you cut through it now, on one of those impatient trains
making hasty tracks for elsewhere, its back is turned disdainfully,
its garden hedges prickly, its householders otherwise preoccupied.

As far as can be seen, your traitorous face – reflected in carriage
glass – doesn't ring the faintest of cathedral bells and only the family
headstone is still willing to claim you unbegrudgingly as its own.

You remember a town where lives seemed doomed to fail: factories
to pack up, able-bodied men to bail out for England and its building
     sites.
Now even a nail-bar thrives, the Chamber of Commerce outlook is
     upbeat.

Any sadness you feel when leaving is on your side alone, crocodile tears
as far as the place is concerned; yet you always quicken to its name
emblazoned on a container truck, its accent picked out in the city crowd.

Vigil

Life is too short to sleep through.
Stay up late, wait until the sea of traffic ebbs,
until noise has drained from the world
like blood from the cheeks of the full moon.
Everyone else around you has succumbed:
they lie like tranquillised pets on a vet's table;
they languish on hospital trolleys and friends' couches,
on iron beds in hostels for the homeless,

under feather duvets at tourist B & Bs.
The radio, devoid of listeners to confide in,
turns repetitious. You are your own voice-over.
You are alone in the bone-weary tower
of your bleary-eyed, blinking lighthouse,
watching the spillage of tide on the shingle inlet.
You are the single-minded one who hears
time shaking from the clock's fingertips
like drops, who watches its hands
chop years into diced seconds,
who knows that when the church bell
tolls at 2 or 3 it tolls unmistakably for you.
You are the sole hand on deck when
temperatures plummet and the hull
of an iceberg is jostling for prominence.
Your confidential number is the life-line
where the sedated long-distance voices
of despair hold out muzzily for an answer.
You are the emergency services' driver
ready to dive into action at the first
warning signs of birth or death.
You spot the crack in night's façade
even before the red-eyed businessman
on look-out from his transatlantic seat.
You are the only reliable witness to when
the light is separated from the darkness,
who has learned to see the dark in its true
colours, who has not squandered your life.

Before

A carpet-cushioned
hush as you arrive
at the marble check-in desk,
bringing your watch
up to speed on local time.
Registration forms.
Credit card impress.
The porter – cabin bags,
suitcase in tow – shows you
to your made-up room.
Elevator pings.
Linen trolleys.
Furniture polish spume.

                    *

Alone in your designated office,
you take in the back-of-buildings view,

trying to make vague sense of the procedures
set out in the manual you've been handed.

This first day grows longer by the minute.
A telephone keeps ringing in your predecessor's name.

                    *

When the morning presenter enters,
the studio door shuts behind her
with an emphatic thud, leaving her alone
with a flood of requests in that sealed
and leakproof capsule, an astronaut
awaiting the producer's countdown.

Bungalows where house lights come
on stream, as curtains fall on dreams,
will soon grow fully attuned.
Workers with radio-alarms will be roused
by her call to take up their arms and rise,
her voice getting carried away above farms,
bedsitters, office blocks, transmitter masts
like fir trees in which a dawn chorus sings.

*

Ahead of schedule,
the truck driver breaks for freedom
near the city's edge.

From car level, what you glimpse
is a pencil perched behind
an ear; a glint of steel

from a cigarette lighter,
a tabloid like a docket
in a swarthy hand.

*

The apprentice hairdresser
happy in blonde streaks of sun
could wait outdoors all morning
for her agitated boss to open late,
breathlessly confessing to a mislaid key.

*

A show apartment.
Unoccupied space like unpolluted air.
Fresco-fresh bright walls.

White couch, chintz drapes.
State-of-the-art prints.
Spotless ceramic splashbacks.
Unworked marble worktops.
The steely assurance
of the self-cleaning hob.

*

The day approaches.
You begin to fold some clothes
in readiness: the pink towelling
dressing gown, the sensible
nightdresses, still in cellophane.
You try to recall what kind
of bedroom slippers are the norm
and must make sure to jot down
health insurance numbers
and other facts you'll need
when you sit in Admissions
with your holiday holdall
pretending to read old horoscopes
in tatty cast-off magazines.

*

The full-fry pall envelops you
half-way down the fluffy
stairs-carpet to the hall.
In the breakfast room,
another couple, seated next
to sports trophies, wedding photos,
is swapping sibilants.
Crunch of corn flakes, toast.
Clash of cup and saucer.
Splenetic fat is heard

hissing in the pan
as the chatty landlady
appears from the kitchen
clutching hot plates
with a cotton dishcloth,
wishing you good morning,
hoping you both slept well.

*

In staid, straight-backed velvet chairs
around a gleaming convent dining table,
your school debating team has five minutes
to prepare its case against the motion.
Practised scales leak from upstairs.
Corridor giggles are inflamed by a nun's shushes.
You block-letter notes on prompt-cards.
There is no arguing with the clock.

*

Before the paint roller
makes its sweeping statements,
lisping gummily along,
the room is stripped down;
picture marks are like the traces
of discarded clothes.
The modesty of furniture
is safeguarded by sheets.

*

Check the plates are heating.
Flick the speck from a champagne glass.
Pick a loose thread off your sequinned dress.
Straighten your necklace.

Adjust your hair in the mirror one more time.
Steady the candles in their silver holders.
Start, as if taken by surprise,
when the doorbell rings.

*

Lights in the Community Centre
generate excitement.
What's up?
What's on tonight?
A Lions Club AGM?
A ballroom dancing class?
A drama group rehearsal?
A youth disco?
A whist drive?

*

As you climb the arts centre steps,
expectation mounting,
the organiser forewarns you
that the body count
is lower than anticipated.
You make your entrance,
nodding to the few acquaintances
who brave the austere seats.

*

Riffle through your notes.
Repeatedly clear your throat.
Skim a promotion brochure.
Try to look composed
when the bubbly

broadcast assistant arrives
to lead you to the studio.

*

Before proceeding
with my business,
I eat lunch in a small
malt-smelling pub
well off the beaten track
and, though my fate
lies with the main road,
I linger in this backwater,
storing for future use
the view I had
until now relegated
to a background detail,
a windscreen saver.
I will be glancing
over my shoulder
as I speed away.

Index of Titles

Some new and recent poetry from Anvil